Good Food from
Mrs. Sundberg's Kitchen

by Holly Harden

Adventure Publications, Inc.
Cambridge, MN

Dedication

For Rosie and Virginia

Acknowledgments

Mrs. Sundberg and I are most grateful to the following, without whom this cookbook would not be open on the kitchen counter:

The good people at Adventure Publications for their hard work and dedication

Tim Trost, the artist whose work has brought life, past and present, to these pages

Garrison Keillor and our dear friends at *A Prairie Home Companion* for saying "yes" and lifting it up

The Forest Lake Writers' Workshop, for their enduring support and encouragement

Mr. Sundberg and the kids, for providing feedback by cleaning their plates, or not

The women of the church, who set the bar high

And all the people along the way who bring a dish to pass and share the recipe, who run out to get more butter or whatever else is missing, and who stay—those few good souls—to do the dishes and clean up after the gathering

Illustrations by Timothy T. Trost/www.timtrost.com

Cover and book design by Jonathan Norberg

10 9 8 7 6 5 4 3 2 1

Copyright 2014 by Holly Harden
Published by Adventure Publications, Inc.
820 Cleveland Street South
Cambridge, MN 55008
1-800-678-7006
www.adventurepublications.net
Printed in China
ISBN: 978-1-59193-448-6

Good Food from

Mrs. Sundberg's Kitchen

. . . .

Table of Contents

Foreword by Garrison Keillor

The pleasure of fine dining has worn thin for me, I must admit. I realized this the other day when I sat in a nouveau-something restaurant and gazed at the menu and felt a craving for a grilled cheese sandwich and a bowl of chili. Not a gourmet chili with essence of cilantro and oil of palm and swirls of liquefied avocado and a partridge in a pear tree but the kind you used to get at Woolworth's lunch counter, served by a woman with a hairnet who looked like your great-aunt.

I look at the cookbooks in our pantry from back in my gourmet days when I was ambitious to make remoulade of blanched snow peas and a walleye seviche and seared squirrel cheeks on a bed of lichen with an effusion of asphalt, and I know those days will not come again. I used to be a man with twenty-four different kinds of oregano! I fought with other men over the comparative virginity of our respective olive oils. I once showed a man named Jake how to shave parmigiano thin and translucent as parmigiano should be shaved and he felt insulted and shoved me away and we rolled around on the kitchen floor, punching and kicking and gouging each other. Now we're best friends. Once I shot a man in Reno who told me that my dressing needed more vinegar. He was wrong about that. Dead wrong.

And then suddenly it was all over. I threw a dinner party for twelve and made gazpacho and risotto and tacos and osso buco and a gateau of Jell-O with marshmallows and served it with a Barolo and when the guests left, delirious with pleasure, I put my whisk away and never looked back. It wasn't fun anymore. A man comes to a point in life when he decides that he doesn't have to make the best risotto in town. People still ask me what is the secret of my risotto and I tell them, "That part of my life is behind me now." I'm packing up the cookbooks, the long-handled copper sauce pans, the graters and grinders and blenders and special spatulas, and giving them to the Salvation Army, because the simple truth is that I like Spanish rice. Macaroni and cheese is good, the manna that God gave to the Christian people in the wilderness, which is where we are still living. And there are so many ways to make meatloaf.

I never knew fine cuisine that could make up for bad company, or good conversation that was spoiled by mediocre cooking. That's my opinion and I have suffered through some bad company to reach it. People who came to the table with long monologues about piffle and hogwash and all of your hard work marinating the grouper overnight in lilac blossoms and oil of chamomile and blowing cigar smoke on it every two hours is pretty much for naught. Whereas I have heard some wonderful stories over buttermilk pancakes and molasses.

This is a book of excellent dishes that Mrs. Sundberg has made, and they reflect the values of Midwestern cooking, including Lake Wobegon. *Goodness* is one value and *heartiness* is another and also the idea that artifice cannot make up for poor character. Weary cynical tomatoes and wizened cucumbers cannot be made passable by tricking them out with exotic spices from the East. It pays to be close to the source of your supplies. And one more thing: you won't read this in other cookbooks, but it's important— the essential requirement for true appreciation of good cooking is *hunger*. Americans tend to overeat and oversnack and come to the table with no real appetite. If you mow the lawn or shovel the walk or ride your bike before a meal, you'll eat with keener pleasure. But you know that.

A Note from Mrs. Sundberg

I grew up a small town in the Midwest, and it makes sense I would land in one. There are good people here, and a lake, a park and a couple churches and several perfect picnic spots. It's my kind of place to be. Together we build bonfires and bring in the hay. We clean up each other's yards after storms, plow each other's driveways and shovel each other's walks. We gather for funerals and graduations and weddings and births, and we gather for coffee, and gather for no reason at all, and when we do, we always bring a little something—flowers from the garden, or bath salts or wine, but mostly we bring food.

I remember going to Great Uncle Ray's for the Annual Fish Boil when I was a kid. Great Aunt Frieda always wore an apron, the bibbed kind, with flowers, and there were long tables covered with flowered plastic, filled with pasta and Jell-O salad and rolls, pickles and beets and potato salad and rice pudding. There were cakes with homemade chocolate frosting, and platters of cherry and maple and pumpkin bars. I remember standing there, among my family, holding a heavy-duty paper plate, waiting for Uncle Ray to holler, "Come 'n get it!" and start scooping chunks of fish and potato from the giant pot of boiling water. Nothing else tasted as good as that boiled fish drenched with melted butter.

And then there were those Easter breakfasts at church, and the rows of egg bake lined up on the counter, and the platters piled high with sausage and cinnamon rolls. The smell of coffee filled the air and families sat together talking and laughing long after the food was gone. Funerals were like that, only we ate ham and tuna and egg sandwiches, and there were hotdishes and plates of pickles. I remember the smell of venison kabobs on the grill as we sat together on August evenings at the picnic table in our backyard, and I remember eating chipped beef dip on Christmas Eve while waiting to open gifts. And there were bags filled with chocolate chip cookies Mom sent with us when my brothers and I rode out to the rope swing under the river bridge.

One of my fondest memories is of watching my mother's forearms as she stirred cookie dough with a wooden spoon in a giant stoneware bowl. She was young, and intent, and rarely used measuring spoons. She taught me what a teaspoon looks like in the cupped palm of my hand, and that a quarter teaspoon is a heavy pinch. I learned to cook mostly by watching her, and my father and grandmothers, and by asking a lot of questions. Dad taught me how to make the best fish chowder, and from my grandmothers I learned about bread and cakes, cookies and pies. I never aspired to be a chef, but I did want to make food as good and simple as theirs. So I paid attention and asked for copies of recipes, and I practiced.

I'm still practicing. I found a recipe last week for fish tacos, and was all excited and made a huge production of it all, and somehow they didn't taste right. The kids loved the fish part, but the rest went to the compost heap. That's how it goes. The good ones I keep, like the recipe for chicken hotdish from my grandma's funeral, the one that tastes like comfort itself. I'll make it later this week for the new neighbors moving in down the street. And my favorite recipe for pizza dough I'm using tomorrow when the kids' cousins come for a visit. See how that goes over, along with some sugar cookie cutouts shaped like dogs and suns. We'll decorate them together.

Labor Day Weekend at the Cabin

· · · · · · · · · · · · ·

Flapjacks Supreme

Hobo Dinners on the Grill

Mrs. Sundberg's Dad's Easy
Beer Batter for Fish

Homemade Blueberry Muffins

Rhubarb Pie

Made blueberry muffins on Saturday, and they were pretty good. I had the radio on, and while I listened I imagined myself all sprawled out on the deck of a ship, with nothing to do but breathe in the ocean air and listen to the birds and feel the lull of the ship and the mild vibrations of Mr. Sundberg snoring next to me. Makes me shiver a bit. Not my husband's snoring, but the thought of floating out on the ocean with no dryer buzzer going off in the background and no one asking, "Aren't you making bars today?"

No, I'm not making bars today. It's not my destiny. My destiny has to do with a house on a lake with a big front porch and some rose bushes and pine trees. My destiny includes a boat (I don't care much whether it's a canoe or a bass boat or a pontoon, but now that I think about it I think I'd go for the pontoon), a swing on that big ol' open porch, and whitecaps on those lake waves as often as the North Wind pleases. There's a big ol' oven in the kitchen, and toilet seats that don't pinch your butt, and a bed with a soft, even mattress and windows with shutters to fling open in the morning and lean out like in that aftershave commercial.

There are photos all 'round of everything between now and then, and the phone doesn't ring; it hums "Hail, Hail, The Gang's All Here" and I hear echoes of the kids' voices in every room. And yes, there are bars. Of course. How could bars not appear in my destiny? Chocolate cherry bars, mostly-baked chocolate chip bars, lemon bars. Bars every day, or cookies, or a good loaf of cranberry orange bread.

Lord, Almighty. I'm going to have to make a pan of bars. A cruise, a nap with Mr. S on the deck, my dream house on a Minnesota lake, that enormous porch with a view of the sun falling away . . . it can all wait. The kids will be in from the beach soon, and it's been a while since I've made those peanut butter bars, the ones with the chocolate topping. Something to be said for the moment, this moment, and life within it.

Flapjacks Supreme

4 eggs
2 cups buttermilk
2 T melted butter
2 cups flour

2 tsp sugar
½ tsp salt
2 tsp baking powder

Separate eggs into two medium-sized bowls: whites in one; yolks in the other. Beat whites until stiff; set aside. Beat yolks. Add buttermilk and melted butter. Combine flour, sugar, salt and baking powder; add to buttermilk mixture. Blend well. Fold in whites. Fry 2-3 inch wide pancakes on lightly greased griddle. Serve with sausage or bacon. Batter is even better a day or two later.

Hobo Dinners on the Grill

1-1½ lb, thawed hamburger
1-2 medium, washed and thinly
   sliced potatoes
1-2 medium carrots

1 large sweet onion
4-8 oz, washed mushrooms
A bit of butter for each
Salt and pepper, to taste

Mold hamburger into 4-6 patties; place each on a large square of heavy-duty aluminum foil. Arrange thinly sliced potatoes, carrots, onions, mushrooms, and/ or whatever vegetables you desire on top of each hamburger patty. Add a bit of butter to each, and salt and pepper. You might add a bit of barbecue or steak sauce if that's your kind of thing. Seal foil well, and place each hobo dinner on the grill. Cover grill and cook, checking after 15 minutes. Depending on the grill, cook half hour to 45 minutes, or to your liking.

Mrs. Sundberg's Dad's Easy Beer Batter for Fish

1 can beer, dark is best, like
   red or dark ale
1 egg
⅓ cup flour
⅓ cup Bisquick

½ tsp salt
Dash or two pepper
Paprika
Garlic powder, optional
1 lb fish fillets

Pour ⅓ to ½ can beer in mixing bowl (don't waste it, you can add more later). Stir beer with whisk, and let stand. Stir in egg—beat with whisk or fork.

Add ⅓ cup flour and ⅓ cup Bisquick, ½ tsp. salt, some pepper, and a few shakes of paprika. Mix well. Add more beer as necessary to make a thin batter. (Some also like to add a few shakes of garlic powder to the batter.)

Add fish, and thoroughly coat with batter, shaking off the excess. Fry in oil at 375. Cook 'til golden brown; fish will float when done. Consume remainder of beer with the fish, fried potatoes and green beans. Consume as many more beers as necessary to make you feel as convivial as the occasion warrants. Best when served at a cabin and shared with people you love.

Homemade Blueberry Muffins

1¾ cups flour
¼ cup sugar
2½ tsp baking powder
¼ tsp nutmeg
1 egg

¾ cup milk
⅓ cup oil
1 cup blueberries
A sprinkle of sugar

Mix dry ingredients together. Make a well in center. Add egg, milk and oil. Stir gently. Fold in 1 cup fresh blueberries. Fill 11 muffin cups to ¾ full in tin. Sprinkle lightly with sugar. Bake at 425 for 15-19 minutes or until light brown and center springs back when touched.

Rhubarb Pie

3 cups thinly sliced rhubarb
2 eggs
1½ cup sugar
2 T tapioca

¼ tsp salt
¼ tsp nutmeg
Butter

Line an 8-inch pie tin or plate with your favorite pie crust. Fill with rhubarb. Beat eggs, and stir in remaining ingredients. Pour egg mixture over rhubarb, dot with a bit of butter, and cover with top crust, sealing and crimping edges. Slit top crust here and there, and sprinkle with sugar. Bake at 375 for 45 minutes or until crust is golden and fruit comes bubbling out of slits. Cool.

Back to School

· · · · · · · · · · · ·

Barbecues

Homebaked Macaroni and Cheese

Homemade Ranch Fries

Apple Dip

The Peanut Butter Cookie

Made barbecues on Saturday, and they were pretty good. I'd just gotten back from what I believe was the final trip to the store for school items. The load included folders, juice, granola bars, laundry detergent, a shoe organizer, socks and underwear. Lots of underwear. I don't know why it is the start of school requires new underwear but it does. I always thought of underwear for special occasions as an adult thing, but perhaps school starting is enough of an occasion. Anyway, it's good to head out into the unknown with a few new things and to be well-supplied and geared up. The kids are officially prepared. Materially, anyway. Need to practice getting up earlier these next few days.

Emotional preparation is another story.

They feel apprehensive, I think. Nervous. Not sure of what Day One will bring, not certain about who it is they are, themselves, venturing out. Not entirely convinced that It's All Good. Growing up isn't in the Top Ten List of Easy Things. Frankly, it's painful. Takes up a lot of energy and time. And room. But it's inevitable, necessary and, ultimately, good.

I thought I'd stop growing when I became a grown-up. I'm not sure when I became one, to be honest. And it seems when I did, the growing didn't stop; it shifted gears. Now I not only get to keep growing, but also to nudge along three young people who often look to me for assurance, advice, comfort. "Am

I OK?" my son asked today. He's been counting days, I think. "Yes, you are," I told him. "How do you know?" he questioned. "Because I know," I said.

I do know. Whatever makes you grow is gonna hurt somehow. It might take you away from someone you love, might keep you from paying bills on time, might make you work out more often or eat foods that will lower your cholesterol. It might force you to draft a budget or buy a wheelchair or meet with the person you least wish to see. Might have to forgo the new boots, sell the house, or sign a legal document. Might have to grieve an unexpected death, take a class, enroll in a program, or recover from 26 hours of labor. Or sign up for an online dating service in your sixties. Or get up on stage. On and on.

No, you don't need new underwear to meet the next challenge. But it can't hurt, really. Underwear is good. Growth is good. Always has been. Always will be.

Barbecues

1 lb hamburger
Onion, optional
1 can tomato soup
2 T barbecue sauce (Sweet Baby
  Ray's is pretty good)

1 T mustard
2 T ketchup
2 T vinegar
¼ cup brown sugar

Brown hamburger. If you're an onion person, chop one up and brown it along with the hamburger. Add soup and remaining ingredients to your liking; I often add more ketchup and brown sugar. Simmer for an hour or two. Serve on fresh buns.

Homebaked Macaroni and Cheese

3 T butter
¼ cup flour
1 tsp salt
½ tsp dry mustard
¼ tsp pepper
2½ cups milk

2 cups cheddar cheese, grated
½ lb Velveeta cheese
1 cup mozzarella cheese
1 (16 oz) box elbow
  macaroni, cooked
Paprika

In large saucepan over medium heat, melt butter. Stir in flour, salt, mustard and pepper until smooth; remove from heat. Stir in milk until smooth, return to burner and continue stirring for 10 minutes until thick; remove from heat. Add 1½ cups cheddar cheese, Velveeta cheese and mozzarella cheese and stir until melted (you may need to place on burner to fully melt cheese). Put cooked macaroni in a greased casserole dish, pour cheese mixture over and mix well. Lightly sprinkle paprika and leftover cheddar on top. Bake at 375 degrees for 20 minutes.

Homemade Ranch Fries

4-6 large potatoes
Olive oil
Parmesan cheese

Garlic salt
Pepper

Wash potatoes and slice lengthwise into 6 or 8 wedges each. Place in a bowl and drizzle several tablespoons of olive oil over. Mix until well-coated. Sprinkle desired amount of Parmesan cheese and garlic salt over, and a little pepper, and mix again. (You can also use a store-bought seasoning mixture such as Mrs. Dash or Lawry's.)

Pour potato wedges onto a foil-covered (lightly grease the foil) jelly roll pan or cookie sheet, separating the slices so they're evenly distributed. Bake at 500 for 15 minutes, turning fries over with a spatula about halfway through.

Serve with burgers or fish or chicken and ranch dressing for a dip. Variations include sprinkling shredded cheese and/or crumbled bacon over before baking. Fries are done when lightly browned and fork slides in easily.

Let the kids, or the grandkids, break the eggs into the bowl while you're baking. A little eggshell never hurt anyone, and good cooks have to start somewhere. When you're done, invite them to wipe the dishes while you wash. Dishwashers don't allow for good conversation.

Apple Dip

8 oz cream cheese
¾ cup brown sugar
¼ cup white sugar
1 tsp vanilla
½ to 1 cup peanut butter
Sliced apples and bananas

Cream first five ingredients together, and serve with sliced apples and bananas.

The Peanut Butter Cookie

1 cup butter
1 cup sugar
1 cup brown sugar
1 cup peanut butter
2 eggs

A couple drops of vanilla
3 cups flour
1 tsp baking soda
Couple of dashes of salt
Chocolate chips, optional

Cream butter with sugars; add peanut butter and stir well. Mix in eggs and vanilla. Add flour, soda and salt and stir until well blended. Drop in walnut-sized blobs onto an ungreased sheet and criss-cross with a fork dipped in flour. Bake at 350 for 6-10 min or so, depending on how soft you like 'em. Chocolate chips are good in this recipe, too.

A Saturday Evening Potluck in September

· · · · · · · · · · · ·

Sweet Vidalia Cheese Dip

Meatloaf Surprise

Twice Baked Potatoes to Your Liking

Roasted Vegetables

Apple Crisp

Made apple crisp on Saturday, and it was pretty good. With the onset of autumn, and darkening skies and a bit of rain over the weekend, the ol' mood has been a bit low and all it took was "Blue Eyes Cryin' in the Rain" playin' on the radio to get me going. Not an All-out Cry, mind you. A few tears for a song that takes me way back, to when I was a girl and life was simple and things like first kisses and big parts in musicals took up my time and attention. A time when I pretended to be asleep on the couch hoping my father still might have it in him to carry me upstairs and tuck me into my bed.

No, the All-out Cry came Friday afternoon. I suppose you could chalk it up to the weather, which was somewhere between drizzle and rain. No thunder and lightning, no drama—just a steady steamy stream of water pouring on down. The windows in my van kept fogging up in the midst of my errands, people were generally quiet and without a smile, and I felt lacking in something. Courage, maybe. Or strength. Or whatever it is that sustains those always-happy people. Not that I aspire to constant joy, but there are days when I feel its absence like we all do, and Friday was one of 'em. Of course, it could have been a hormonal thing, or the fact that the kids have been a bit more needy than usual with the start of school and puberty and all. Or maybe I was just having a really crappy day. I'd lost my umbrella, my hair was out of control, and I couldn't seem to catch up with myself.

I was fine as I visited the bank, the post office, the gas station, and the movie store. I even hummed as I wandered through Target. I suppose I didn't need the three large bags of peanut butter M&Ms or seven boxes of Kleenex. Nope. But I bought them. And I bought a notebook too. I took it all out to the car and loaded it up and that's when I came undone. The tears started, and they weren't stopping. I drove to the back of the lot, locked the doors, left the music on, took off my shoes, and climbed to the back seat of the van where I wrapped myself in a plaid wool stadium blanket. For a good hour, I lay there with the windows steamed up, crying about everything, and nothing in particular.

They say that crying releases hormones and painkillers and rids you of the toxins that build up in your body. It cleans you out. It's like a built-in rinse cycle. Women cry 64 times a year and men, 17. It's healthy. And it feels good. Felt good to me, anyway, all curled up in my van with the rain beating on the roof on a Friday afternoon somewhere between summer's end and the first leaves of autumn.

Sweet Vidalia Cheese Dip

- 2 cups mayonnaise
- 2 cups shredded Parmesan cheese
- 2 cups shredded sweet Vidalia onions

Mix. Pour into casserole. Bake at 350 for 45 min, or until you can't wait any longer.

Meatloaf Surprise

1 lb hamburger
4 slices bread, shredded into
　small pieces
1 egg
1 egg white
½ tsp oregano
½ tsp basil
1 T ketchup

2 tsp mustard
1 T barbecue sauce (optional)
Dashes of salt and pepper
¾ cup brown sugar
Ketchup
6-8 oz cheese, sliced or grated
Miscellaneous "surprises"

In large bowl, mix raw hamburger, bread, egg, egg white, and seasonings until well-blended. (This works best if you use your hands.)

Cover bottom of 9x5 loaf pan (or your favorite loaf pan) with brown sugar (about ½-¾ cup). Squirt ketchup in a grid pattern over brown sugar until it is about half covered (½ cup or so). Press about ⅔ of the meat mixture onto the brown sugar/ketchup base. Create a trench in the meat by pressing a large spoon down the center. Fill with cheese of your choice. If you wish, add some chopped green pepper or mushrooms or be creative. Press down, and cover and seal trench with remaining meat mixture.

Bake covered at 350 for 30 min. Remove cover. Bake another 20 minutes or until desired darkness. Remove from oven. Let sit 5 minutes, loosen edges with a spatula, and carefully invert onto a platter. Your meatloaf will be covered with a tangy sweet sauce. Makes good sandwiches as leftovers.

Twice Baked Potatoes to Your Liking

6 large, whole russet or Yukon
  Gold potatoes
Sour cream (about a cup for
  6 potatoes)
Butter
Salt
Pepper

2 cups shredded cheddar cheese
Bacon bits
1-2 T Milk
Parsley
Paprika
Green onions, optional

Wash potatoes and prick with fork. Bake at 375 until fork enters smoothly, about an hour, longer depending on potato size. Let cool a bit, and scoop out the entire inside of potato into a bowl, leaving skins intact.

Add to potatoes—in amounts to your liking—sour cream, butter, salt, pepper, ½ cup shredded cheddar cheese, and bacon bits. Blend together. (The consistency can range anywhere from being somewhat chunkier to exactly as smooth as mashed potatoes). Add a tablespoon or two of milk if mixture seems dry. A few green onions are also optional.

Spoon mixture back into potato skins and top with remaining cheese and whatever else sounds good. Bake on foil in a 9x13 cake pan at 375 until the cheese is melted.

For added color, sprinkle chopped parsley and paprika on top as a garnish.

Wear aprons. You can wipe your hands on them, and they're really kind of sexy.

Roasted Vegetables

Cauliflower
Red pepper
Green pepper
Olive oil
Salt
Pepper

Cut vegetables into bite-sized pieces. Place on a foil-covered 11x13 jelly roll pan. Drizzle with olive oil. Stir around to coat all pieces. Roast in oven at 350-375, stirring occasionally, until vegetables are done to your liking. Season with salt and pepper. You may add other vegetables as you wish, but this combination is particularly tasty.

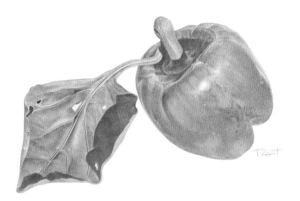

Apple Crisp

10-12 apples, your favorite varieties for baking
¾ cup sugar
1-2 T cinnamon

Peel and slice up apples. Go for a mix of tart and sweet if you like, or all one kind. Put 'em in a 9x13 buttered pan and sprinkle with about ¾ cup sugar and 1-2 T cinnamon.

Now for the topping, there are two ways to go: doughy and sweet, or oaty and spicy.

Doughy

½ cup butter, softened   1 cup flour
1 cup brown sugar   1 T cinnamon, ¼ t salt

I have doubled this topping in this recipe and received applause.

Oaty

11 T butter   1 T cinnamon
1⅓ cup brown sugar   1 T allspice
1¼ cup flour   ¼ t salt
1 cup oats

Whichever topping you choose, combine ingredients and sprinkle over apples. Then, bake at 350 for 30 minutes or until light brown.

Serve with ice cream. Or whipped cream. Enjoy!

The House to Yourself

· · · · · · · · · · · ·

Fried Egg Sandwich

Creamed Chipped Beef on Toast

Baked Apple Pancake

Buffalo Chicken Dip

Molasses Creams

Made a baked apple pancake on Saturday, and it was pretty good. The kids were out with friends and I was alone for a while, having spent the week running two kids here and there and a day visiting the third at college, and the house was quiet except for the radio playing a sweet song about a mandolin player. I generally enjoy being alone, but once school starts, the quiet shifts a bit, and it shifted. All it took was that bus pulling up one September morning at 7:12 a.m., the two younger ones climbing on, and a lurch as the bus pulled away. And there I was in a house filled with echoes.

The first definition of "lonesome" listed in the dictionary includes the word "dejected"—a result of a lack of companionship. I was not dejected, but I did feel solitary, which is part of definition number four. Lone. Solitary. Yes. I got to thinking about that word last week when my mother called to tell me of a PBS special about a man who canoed to a remote part of Alaska and lived alone there for more than thirty years. He was looking for a lonesome place to spend some time, do some fishing. Or just be. My mother was so taken with the idea of a lonesome place as something one might seek out, and called to ask where mine might be.

There are trees in my Lonesome, trees along a meadow, and a lake nearby. The wind always blows there, and the leaves shimmer silver in that wind, and the sun is warm. When it storms in my Lonesome, the skies are Old Testament and the rain falls hard. I walk there. I can cry if I want to, or sing something or just walk. Now and then I lay myself down in the golden meadow grass and make an "X" with my body and close my eyes and think about nothing at all for a good twenty minutes. It works for me. Lonesome smells like fresh grass and oak leaves, and there's nothing there to fear. Don't think I'll spend thirty years there, but I'll visit now and then. It's familiar to me, like the sound of pots and pans and alarm clocks, and the taste of fresh bread and the way a hot bath feels after a good long day.

Fried Egg Sandwich

2 eggs
Salt and pepper, to taste
2 slices bread
Cheese of your choice, optional

Break eggs into frying pan. Gently break yolks and spread over whites. Add a couple of spoonsful of water. Put cover on pan. Cook until eggs are the way you like them. Salt and pepper to taste. Cut eggs to fit the bread. Layer: bread, egg, bread. Eat. Ketchup for dipping is optional. For added comfort, add cheddar or provolone cheese to sandwich and fry both sides.

Creamed Chipped Beef on Toast

2 (2 oz) packages of sliced beef, cut up as you like
Sliced bread

Cream Sauce

2 T butter
2 T flour
Salt, as desired

Dash of pepper
1½ cups milk

Melt butter in a small saucepan. Stir in flour, salt and pepper. Add milk all at once. Cook over medium heat until thick and bubbly, stirring all the while. Add sliced beef. Cook and stir one minute more. Serve over your favorite bread, toasted.

Baked Apple Pancake

4 eggs
1½ cups milk
½ tsp salt
2 T sugar
2 cups white flour, sifted
3 tart apples, peeled, cored and sliced
½ cup sugar
1 T cinnamon
3 T butter
1 container cream

Beat the eggs until thick; add the milk, salt and sugar. Sift in the flour, mixing it well. Let batter stand for half an hour. Meanwhile, prepare the apples and cinnamon sugar (½ cup sugar mixed with 1 T cinnamon). Butter well two 8- or 9-inch round cake pans and sprinkle with part of the cinnamon sugar. Arrange the sliced apples in the pans and sprinkle with the remaining cinnamon sugar and dot with butter. Pour the pancake batter over the apples, dividing it evenly between the pans. Bake at 375 for 30 minutes or until the top is golden brown and set. Cut into wedges and serve plain or with cream poured over each serving. Makes 2 huge pancakes.

Buffalo Chicken Dip

8 oz cream cheese
4 oz buffalo hot sauce
4 oz ranch dressing

6 oz shredded cheddar
8 oz cooked chopped chicken breast

Mix ingredients together and microwave on high for a minute or so. Remove and stir. Microwave on high again until dip is hot. You may also bake at 350 for 15-30 minutes, stirring once. Serve with Fritos or crackers or chips.

Molasses Creams

¼ cup shortening
½ cup sugar
1 egg
½ cup molasses
2 cups flour
½ tsp soda

½ tsp salt
1 tsp ginger
¾ tsp cinnamon
½ tsp cloves
½ cup water

Cream together shortening and sugar; beat in egg, and add molasses and stir. Combine dry ingredients and add alternately with water. Mix well. Drop with teaspoon onto greased cookie sheet.

Bake at 400 about 8 minutes. Frost with powdered sugar frosting or cream cheese frosting. (For frosting recipe, see page 56.) Makes 3 dozen or so cookies.

Oktoberfest

· · · · · · · · · · · · ·

Reuben Dip

Creamy Kielbasa and Kraut

Grandma's Potato Pancakes

German Sweet and Sour Red Cabbage

Lazy Dazy Cake

Made kielbasa and kraut on Saturday, and it was pretty good. The kids and I had dinner early, and after I washed the dishes, I headed out to pick up Mr. Sundberg at the airport. I'd planned a bit ahead and had his favorite dessert waiting for him on the counter, still nearly warm, and he was so happy about that. Apple Caramel Crisp, with a little extra cinnamon, and some vanilla ice cream on the side.

Mr. Sundberg is not what I'd call ebullient when it comes to sharing his innermost feelings, but he came close that evening as we sat listening to the radio—saying over and over again how good that cake was, and how it was worth the long layover in Chicago and how good it felt to be home and how every time he smelled cinnamon he thought of me. "You're my Spice Girl," he said and I threw a pillow at him and he got up and chased me around the living room. (Which looks much different than it might have twenty years ago, but a chase is a chase.) And then he caught me because I let him and we hugged awhile, pressing our cheeks together, not saying much of anything.

Sometimes words don't work so well. Sometimes they get old, or disappear, and then what do you do? I read a quote a while back, something Sophia Loren said about how cooking is an act of love, "a gift, a way of sharing with others the little secrets—'piccoli segreti'—that are simmering on the burners." She's got something there. "Here's a dessert I made for you," can change the course of someone's day. It says "I love you," yes, but it says other things, too, the little secrets. Like, "I have time for you" and "I know what your favorite things are" and "I want you to experience apple intoxication." And so we busy ourselves in the kitchen, and drive to the airport and home again, and take out the garbage, and play chase. And press our cheeks together, and all that takes us from there to here. And back again.

Reuben Dip

½ cup sauerkraut, drained and chopped
1 (3 oz) pkg cream cheese, softened
1 (8 oz) container sour cream
½ cup grated Swiss cheese
4 oz sliced corned beef, finely diced
2-3 T milk

Combine all ingredients but milk in a small saucepan and heat over low heat until hot. Or microwave in a small bowl for 4 minutes, stirring halfway through. Thin with milk if necessary. Serve with rye or pumpernickel breadsticks.

Creamy Kielbasa and Kraut

1 ring smoked kielbasa
1 can cream of mushroom soup
1 can sauerkraut

Slice smoked kielbasa and fry up in a skillet. Drain fat, and add a can of cream of mushroom soup. Stir, and add a can of sauerkraut, drained. Stir it up again and heat until bubbly. Serve in a bowl, on toast, on a bun, whatever.

Grandma's Potato Pancakes

4 large potatoes, grated
2-3 eggs
1 cup milk

1 tsp salt
1 T baking powder
2 T flour

Mix together all ingredients, adding 2 T flour to make batter the thickness of paste. Add more flour if needed. Drop blobs onto butter in frying pan. Cook 'til light brown, flip, press pancake down gently. Fry until side two is light brown and slightly crispy. Serve with butter, sour cream, lingonberries, sauerkraut, just about anything.

German Sweet and Sour Red Cabbage

3-4 slices bacon, cut into
  1 inch pieces
1 head thin sliced red cabbage
1 large sliced onion (red preferred)
2 apples, peeled and sliced

½ cup vinegar
¼ cup packed brown sugar
Salt and pepper as you wish
Pinches of your favorite spices:
  cinnamon, nutmeg, allspice, ginger

In a large sauce pan, saute bacon until limp but not crisp. Add cabbage, onion and apple slices. Toss to coat with bacon drippings. Cover and simmer until cabbage becomes limp. Add vinegar (red wine, balsamic, or apple cider), sugar and other seasonings. Continue simmering, covered; the longer you simmer, the better the flavor. You may need to add a little more water; check while simmering. Taste and adjust seasoning before serving. Very good leftover and reheated. You may also use honey in place of the brown sugar, about half a cup.

Lazy Dazy Cake

½ cup milk
2 T butter
2 eggs
1 cup sugar
1 tsp vanilla
1 cup flour
1 tsp baking powder
¼ tsp salt

Topping

½ cup butter
¾ cup brown sugar
¼ cup cream (I use milk)
1 cup coconut

Heat ½ cup milk and 2 T butter to a boil in small saucepan or microwave. Set aside. Combine eggs, 1 cup sugar, and vanilla; whisk in flour, baking powder, and salt, and add milk and butter mixture. Continue whisking 'til blended well.

Pour into an 8x8 lightly greased/floured baking pan. Bake 30 minutes at 350. Remove when cake springs back when touched.

While the cake bakes, melt ½ cup butter, ¾ cup brown sugar and cream in small pan on stove. Add 1 cup coconut and stir well.

Pour topping over warm cake, spread evenly, return to oven and broil until tips of coconut are browned.

 Test the freshness of eggs by placing them in a large bowl of cold water. If they float, don't use them.

Halloween Party

· · · · · · · · · · · · · ·

Mrs. Sundberg's Wild Rice Soup

Bacon Cornbread

Caramel Snack Mix

Apple Pie Cake

Witches' Brew

Made wild rice soup on Saturday, and it was pretty good. It was cool out, and very windy, and Stephanie Davis was singing "Harvest Blues" on the radio as I cleaned up the kitchen after a really fine meal of soup and corn bake followed up with my version of that apple cake Dolores Solveson always brings over on Halloween. You know the one.

Her house is just down the street across from the Johnsons, and Dolores has made a habit of bringing cake over while the kids are out trick-or-treating, so they'll have a snack waiting for them when they return. She simply wants the company, and we generally sit and talk a good two hours, answering the door every now and then and passing out candy to the rabbits and the ballerinas and the trolls. It was odd when Dolores didn't show up this year. Every time the doorbell rang and I held out the bowl of candy, I took a gander down the street. I called three times and left three messages. I called Ruth, her best friend, and she said she hadn't heard from her either.

So after the kids were in bed, I grabbed a flashlight and headed on over there. No answer after several knocks, so I tried the door, and it was open and I went in. I didn't even have to holler. There she was, all curled up, her silver-bunned head resting on the arm of the couch. She was wearing a pink gingham apron over a brown dress. There was a bowl of candy and a few wrappers on the coffee table. She was smiling a bit and didn't stir, and I knew that she wasn't about to, either.

To keep a short story short, Dolores had died sometime that afternoon. While I waited for the police to arrive, sitting there holding Dolores' hand, the strangest warmth washed over me. I remembered how she'd planted pralines in her backyard, hoping they would grow, and how she'd always wanted to fly a plane, and how deeply she missed Leroy, her husband, after he died of flu complications a year or so ago. And I remembered how Dolores always said that change is good, and that the seasons really are quite a blessing. They give us something to focus on, something to remind us we're moving forward, not back. She always said, "Imagine what it would be like if nothing ever changed." "We'd all be lumps," she said, "and I'm not down with that movement. I've got places to go." That's what brought me to smiling on Saturday, when the moon was a sliver and the children found their mittens ahead of time. There were flurries in the forecast, and they didn't get here 'til Monday, but they got here. Now I have to find the shovel. The big red one. Never know what's comin', and I've got places to go.

Mrs. Sundberg's Wild Rice Soup

½ cup uncooked wild rice
1 medium onion, minced or chopped as you wish
2 T butter or margarine
1 quart milk
2 cans cream of potato soup
1 lb Velveeta cheese
Optional: 10 strips crisp bacon, crumbled, or 1 cup cooked, shredded turkey or ham

Mmm, this is going to be good.

Prepare wild rice in separate saucepan according to package directions.
Set aside.

In large 4 qt saucepan or soup pot, saute the onion in the butter until tender.
If you're adding meat, this is a good time to do so. Add milk and potato soup,
adjust heat to medium. When hot, add cheese in chunks, and once the cheese
melts, add the wild rice.

Simmer and serve.
Bacon can be used as a garnish.
For variations, saute mushrooms or green pepper with the onions.

Bacon Cornbread

¾ cup yellow corn meal
1 cup milk
1 cup sour cream
1 cup all-purpose flour
½ tsp soda
2 tsp baking powder
½ tsp salt
¼ cup sugar
1 egg
4 slices crisp bacon, crumbled

Blend cornmeal, milk and sour cream together and set aside for 30 minutes. Sift together other dry ingredients. Beat egg lightly and add to cornmeal mixture. Blend in dry ingredients and beat until just smooth. Add bacon, pour into greased preheated 9-inch square pan. Bake in 375 oven for 15-20 minutes. Serve hot with butter.

Caramel Snack Mix

6 cups Crispix cereal
3 cups Chex Multi-bran cereal
1½ cups peanuts (pecans work, too)
2 sticks of butter
1 cup brown sugar

Combine cereal and nuts in bowl. Set aside.

Melt butter and brown sugar in saucepan. Bring to a boil, turn heat down a bit and continue to boil for 2 minutes, stirring constantly.

Pour sauce over cereal mix and stir gently. Pour mixture onto a jelly roll pan or cookie sheet covered with lightly greased foil.

Bake at 325 degrees for 8 minutes. Stir, and bake for another 8 minutes. Remove from oven and stir again. Cool. Store in an airtight container.

Caution: Do not open airtight container if you have the munchies and are alone in the house.

You don't need a stand-up mixer. You have arms, and you need counter space.

Apple Pie Cake

½ cup butter
2 cups sugar
2 eggs
1 tsp vanilla
2 cups flour
1 tsp cinnamon

½ tsp salt
1 heaping tsp soda
4 T hot water
4 cups chopped apples
½ cup chopped walnuts

Cream together butter and sugar. Beat in eggs and 1 tsp vanilla. Add flour, cinnamon and salt. Mix well. Combine soda and hot water, add and stir. Fold in chopped apples and ½ cup chopped walnuts. (Nuts are generally optional.)

Pour into a lightly greased and floured 9x13 cake pan. Bake at 350 degrees about 45 minutes.

Serve warm with Cool Whip or ice cream or plain. Mmm.

Witches' Brew

6 cups apple cider
1½ tsp cinnamon
½ tsp allspice

¼ tsp powdered cloves
½ cup brown sugar
Cinnamon sticks

Combine in pot on stove. Heat on low for 10 minutes or so. Serve with cinnamon sticks.

Enjoy!

Girls' Weekend While the Guys Are Out Hunting

Sweet Vidalia Tart

Artichoke Dip

Antipasto Bread

Fruit Dip with a Zip

Pumpkin Bars

Made artichoke dip on Saturday, and it was pretty good. Mr. Sundberg was hunting with his buddies, and the kids were with my mother, so I had some girlfriends over for the afternoon and evening. We did some cooking and talking, shared some wine and danced around a bit to good music from the heart of Texas. I've been to Texas only once. When I was young, I went with my grandmother and two aunts, one of whom was moving down there. I have good memories of the place: broiled flounder, warm winds, putt-putt golf, picking up shells in the Gulf of Mexico, and swimming in a hotel pool each night.

Her name was Rosella, and she was a sign reader. We'd pass a sign; she'd read it out loud. And then she'd comment on it. "Harv's Implement. Wonder if Harv's in or he's got his sons working for him like Donny does down at the mercantile. Hmm. Dottie's Bakery. S'pose they got some Bismarcks? Fiona Harke always wanted to have a bakery, but Herman wouldn't have it. Said he needed Fiona at the farm. Worked that woman to her grave. Look, Wichita, 93 miles. I thought we were closer than that. Railroad crossing. I was a young girl when the train started coming through town, and I loved watching it go by. And I watched it every chance I got, 'til the train hit ol' Otis and killed him on the spot. Then my mother said no more. She was that way about parades, too. Wanted me to stand near her, and I'd just as soon join the parade. I must have at least wandered off for my mother to worry herself like that."

Could have been an annoying thing, I suppose, Grandma's sign reading, but I was somehow charmed by it all. Whenever my brothers and I stayed with her and rode along on short trips, Grandma read signs. Now that I think about it, it was one of the few circumstances that led her to talk about her life. Maybe reading those signs gave her a kind of permission to say a little more than she might have said otherwise.

Grandma got a speeding ticket on the way home from Texas, while passing through Missouri. I can't imagine she didn't see the speed limit sign; she must have ignored it. Wisconsin is a long drive from Texas, and Grandma had things to do. She was one of the hardest-working women I've known. I guess you could say she died an outlaw. She never settled that ticket ("Not gonna pay it," she said), and has been wanted in Missouri since. She's been a wanted woman in these parts, too. Mostly 'cause we miss her, and the fattigmand she made each Christmas, and how she waved her wooden spoon around when it was time to eat.

Sweet Vidalia Tart

3 T butter
1 large Vidalia onion, diced
½ cup sour cream
1 (12 oz) can evaporated milk
1 packet dry leek soup mix
3 eggs
1½ cups shredded Monterey Jack cheese
1 (9 inch) deep dish frozen pie crust

Preheat oven to 375.

In a large heavy skillet, saute butter and diced Vidalia onion. Cook until lightly caramelized. Remove from heat and whisk in sour cream. Slowly whisk in evaporated milk. Whisk in dry soup mix until lumps disappear. Whisk in eggs. Mix in the shredded cheese until blended. Spoon mixture into an unbaked pastry. Place pie on a cookie sheet and place in oven.

Bake in preheated oven 40 to 45 minutes; or until a knife inserted comes out clean. Let stand 10 to 15 minutes.

Artichoke Dip

1 can (14 oz) artichoke hearts, drained and chopped
1 pkg (8 oz) feta cheese, crumbled
1 cup mayonnaise
½ cup shredded Parmesan cheese
2 cloves garlic, minced or pressed

Mix all ingredients. Spoon into a pie plate or a shallow baking dish. Bake at 350 for 20-25 minutes or until lightly browned.

Serve with crackers or cubed bread. Makes 2 cups.

Antipasto Bread

2 (11.3 oz) packages refrigerated dinner rolls
¼ cup melted butter
4 oz grated Parmesan (about 1 cup)
6½ oz marinated artichoke hearts, drained

⅓ cup sliced deli hard salami, chopped
⅓ cup chopped red bell pepper
½ cup pitted ripe olives, sliced
2 garlic cloves, pressed

Cut dinner rolls into quarters. Roll in melted butter, then roll in Parmesan. Arrange in greased bundt or fluted pan.

Chop artichokes, salami and pepper. Place in a bowl with olives and garlic. Mix. Sprinkle half the mixture over half the bread. Put more bread over, and add remaining mixture. Sprinkle remaining cheese over. Bake 27-30 min. at 375.

Fruit Dip with a Zip

3 oz instant vanilla
  pudding mix, dry
½ cup Amaretto

½ cup skim milk
8 oz Cool Whip
Strawberries, apples, bananas

Mix together dry pudding mix, Amaretto and milk. Fold in Cool Whip and stir well. Serve with fruit chunks.

Pumpkin Bars

4 eggs
2 cups sugar
2 cups pumpkin
1½ sticks melted butter
2 cups flour
2 tsp baking powder
1 tsp baking soda
½ tsp cinnamon

Frosting

3 oz cream cheese
1 stick softened butter
1 tsp vanilla
1 T milk
3 cups powdered sugar

Blend first four ingredients. Add dry ingredients. Mix well. Pour into a greased and floured 11x16 pan. 9x13 works, too, but it's more of a cake than a bar.

Bake at 400, 25 minutes or until set in middle.

Frost with cream cheese frosting: blend 3 ounces softened cream cheese, 1 stick softened butter, 1 T vanilla and 1 T milk. Add a few drops of milk to soften if necessary. Gradually add three cups powdered sugar; blend well.

Thanksgiving Dinner

. . . .

Holiday Brie

Cream Corn Casserole

Slap It on Your Thigh Sweet Potato Pie

The Great Pumpkin Dessert

Orange Cranberries

A Note on Stuffing

Made pumpkin dessert on Saturday, and it was pretty good. Was, in fact, indulging myself in what a word I just learned best describes: gemütlichkeit (n) (guh-moot-lish-KITE): warm friendliness; comfortableness; coziness. The word came from Anu Garg's "A Word a Day" email I receive, and I could not get it out of my head. I even played the pronunciation over and over again and practiced. I want to know this word.

Important, these months ahead, to seek and find comfort. Important always, I guess, with the storms we face, and the aftermaths. So much comes at a human life, one can't help but think gemütlichkeit a kind of reward, if not a necessity. So often the promise of getting home can get a person through a day.

What's so ironic this time of year, the holidays coming along and all, is that what was once, for me a great source of gemütlichkeit has become nearly the opposite. When I was a child, the shopping after Thanksgiving, maybe a week or so after—sometimes that weekend—in stores all decked out for the holidays, was something I looked forward to and enjoyed with my mom and my brothers. Now? It's called, "Black Friday." The music has already begun, and from what I hear, the sales will begin sometime on Thanksgiving Day. How insane is that?

Come on, people. Thanksgiving is a day out of real time to be with your family, to share your gratitude, to immerse yourself in gemütlichkeit. It's a day to pause. *Not* to rush to You-Know-What-Store(s) to get the giant TV on sale, to get the video game, the latest phone, whatever. You don't even NEED a TV. And I'm guessing not many people you know do, either.

Consider not shopping until the turkey has grown cold. Until it's gone, even. Consider making sure you have enough groceries before Thanksgiving Day on Thursday, then not leaving the house 'til Saturday, Sunday even. Consider simply being. Not buying. Your loved ones don't want stuff. They want you. To be near you and with you. Comfortable, and cozy. That's my plan, and you're invited.

Holiday Brie

1 egg
1 T water
½ of a 17.3 oz pkg puff pastry sheets
(1 sheet), thawed
½-⅓ cup seedless raspberry jam

⅓ cup dried cranberries
¼ cup toasted sliced almonds
1 (13.2 oz) Brie cheese round

Beat egg and water in small bowl. Unfold pastry sheet on lightly floured surface. Roll into 14" square. Spread jam on pastry to within two inches of the edge. Sprinkle with cranberries and almonds, and place cheese in center. Fold pastry up over cheese to cover. Trim excess pastry and gently press to seal. Brush seam with egg mixture, and place seam side down onto baking sheet. Brush further with egg mixture. Bake 20 minutes at 400, or until pastry is golden.

Let stand half an hour or so, and serve with your favorite cracker.

Cream Corn Casserole

1 pkg Jiffy corn bread mix
1 stick melted butter
1 cup sour cream
1 egg

1 can cream corn
1 can whole corn, drained
Peppers and onions, optional

Mix above ingredients in 1½ qt casserole. Bake at 350 for about an hour, or until it's light brown and doesn't jiggle. (You can add peppers and onions for the sake of variety.)

Slap It on Your Thigh Sweet Potato Pie

Filling

6 medium sweet potatoes
1 T cinnamon
½ tsp allspice
2 eggs

1 T vanilla
1 stick of butter
2 cups sugar
Evaporated milk (about 3 T, optional)

Boil the sweet potatoes with skin on until soft. Peel the skin off the potatoes. With a mixer blend the peeled potatoes, cinnamon, allspice, eggs, vanilla, and butter. Slowly add the sugar to your mixture to sweeten the filling to your taste. You may not use the whole two cups of sugar or you may use more. You want to make sure that the mixture has the texture of mashed potatoes. If the mixture is too thick, evaporated milk may be added to get it to the right thickness. Spoon mixture into a lightly greased casserole dish.

Topping

1 stick of butter (melted)
1 cup of brown sugar

1 cup of quick oats
1 cup of chopped pecans

Combine all ingredients in a medium-sized bowl, mix well, and crumble on top of filling. Bake at 350 for about 30-35 minutes.

The Great Pumpkin Dessert

30 oz canned pumpkin
3 eggs
1 cup sugar
12 oz evaporated milk
1 yellow cake mix
2 sticks butter, melted
1 cup chopped pecans (optional)

Combine pumpkin, eggs, sugar and evaporated milk (a large whisk works well). Pour into greased 9x13 pan. Sprinkle dry cake mix evenly over the pumpkin mixture. Drizzle melted butter over the cake mix. Scatter pecans over the top if you wish.

Bake at 350, 60-75 minutes. Let cool a bit and serve with Cool Whip or ice cream.

For a special birthday, make two white cake mixes in one bowl according to directions. Divide batter into smaller bowls for as many colors as you wish, and add a few drops of a different food coloring to each to create an array of colors. Pour colors into two rounds or a 9x13, one color at a time, to create a rainbow effect, or swirled blues and purples, and so on.

Orange Cranberries

1 cup sugar
1 cup fresh squeezed orange juice
2 tsp orange zest
1 (12 oz) pkg fresh cranberries, washed and sorted

Bring sugar, juice, and zest to a boil in a medium saucepan. Add berries. Turn to low and simmer 25 min or so, or until berry skins pop. Chill, and serve with orange garnish.

A Note on Stuffing

I did not include a recipe for stuffing as most people have their own homemade recipe and I am all for that. My favorite base to start with, though, is Brownberry Sage and Onion. Follow the directions, mind you. Start with a cup of sliced celery and a cup of chopped onion sautéed in butter, and go from there. A bit of celery salt helps, and after that, have at it. Throw in some sausage, dried cranberries, baby bella mushrooms, chopped apples. Make it your own! Or leave it as is. Simple.

Enjoy!

After Caroling

· · · · · · · · · · · · ·

Russian Tea

English Toffee

Sweet Laurel's Quick Bread Pudding

Grape Jelly Meatballs

Cheese Ball

Made English toffee on Saturday, and it was pretty good. But that was just the warm-up; I did a little dancin' while I made dinner, too: bacon, egg and cheese sandwiches on toasted English muffins. And some cheesy hash browns on the side, but not pancakes. I often make pancakes or waffles too, but I've felt the need to simplify lately. And not just at mealtime. Seems there's so much, too much, of everything, everywhere. Not that a lot of everything is a bad thing. But really, people. Why not switch gears awhile and pare it down?

And today is a good day to begin. The first of December, the dark month, the corner you round into Christmas and the New Year. Instead of going all out and getting all carried away with the season and working myself into some kind of list-induced-migraine-frenzy, what is it that really matters? Well, instead of sending out Christmas letters to friends and relatives who all pretty much know about me and my life, I'm going to send a few cards to people whom I know could use a piece of real mail. For Christmas Eve, rather than a big ol' dinner with all the fixings, I'll make everyone's favorite hors d'oeuvre, along with a homemade pizza. No new Christmas outfits this year. We *have* nice clothes. Let's wear them. Instead of keeping a grid of numbers and prices and types of gifts for the kids, I'll simply buy a few nice gifts. And one of their gifts will be a trip to the grocery store to pick out groceries for another family, chocolates included. As for all those boxes of decorations and the big plastic Santa and the sacks of garland, well, perhaps we'll leave them and just do up the tree this year, and set out candles all over the house and light them each night.

Things don't have to be so complicated. You can wrap all the gifts in one pattern of wrapping paper and nobody is going to flip out. You don't have to make *all* the Christmas recipes in the box. If you don't make it to the holiday open house at the bank, your account won't be charged. You have one life, people. If it's not crammed full of stuff, it doesn't mean you're wasting it. It means you have time and space. And time is nice. Space is a good thing. Especially if an opportunity to make a snowman comes along.

Russian Tea

2 cups Tang
½ cup instant tea (Lipton with Lemon is good)
2½ cups sugar
1 pkg lemonade mix
2 tsp cinnamon
1 tsp cloves

Combine and store in dry jars with lids. Add 2-3 tsp of hot water per cup when serving.

English Toffee

1 cup butter
1 cup sugar
2 T water
1 T white corn syrup
¾ cup choc chips (I use 1 cup)
Finely chopped walnuts or almonds

Melt butter and add sugar; bring to full rolling boil. Add water and syrup. Cook to soft crack stage (290 degrees), stirring all the time. Have buttered foil ready on a cookie sheet. Spread mixture with rubber spatula. Sprinkle chocolate chips over and spread after they melt a bit. Sprinkle finely chopped nuts over chocolate. Cool. Break apart.

Sweet Laurel's Quick Bread Pudding

3 cups bread cubes (about four slices)
⅓ cup dried fruit (cranberries or raisins), optional
4 eggs, slightly beaten
⅓ cup sugar
1 tsp vanilla
⅛ tsp salt
2 cups milk, scalded
Cinnamon
Nutmeg

Place bread cubes in lightly greased 1 qt casserole. Sprinkle dried fruit over. Combine eggs, sugar, vanilla and salt. Gradually add scalded milk. Pour over bread cubes in casserole, sprinkle with cinnamon and a dash of nutmeg. Bake at 325 for 30-40 minutes, or until a knife poked in center comes out clean. Serve with whipped cream, or your favorite sauce.

Grape Jelly Meatballs

   1 jar chili sauce
   1 cup grape jelly (I use jam, which holds its own a bit better)
   1 pkg meatballs, or make your own

Mix first two ingredients. Place meatballs in a 2½ qt saucepan and pour sauce over. Stir occasionally, and simmer 'til the party begins. Recipe doubles easily.

Cheese Ball

   8 oz cream cheese, softened
   4 oz Velveeta, diced
   1 pkg sliced beef, diced
   Minced onion to taste
   2 T Miracle Whip
   1 tsp garlic powder

Mix all ingredients together; form into a ball. Serve with crackers and a garnish.

Cookie Exchange

· · · · · · · · · ·

The Sugar Cookie

Snowballs

Melt-in-Your-Mouth Sugar Cookies

Mrs. Sundberg's Perfectly Good Spritz

Chocolate Truffle Cookies

Mrs. Jungerberg's Peanut Blossoms

Almond Bark Squares

White Chocolate Chippers

Fattigmand

Chocolate Cherry Cookies

Cranberry Macadamia Nut Cookies

Made chocolate cherry cookies Saturday, and they were pretty good. I'd gotten the house clean and had turned my attention to the closet downstairs where the Christmas gifts have been slowly accumulating. Was doing an inventory of sorts, and it seems I'm about half done with gift-buying for the kids. I pay attention most of the year, and pick up what I can ahead of time when it's on sale, and I'm not in a bad place. Gifts are important, but the spirit of giving is even more so, and when my brothers and our spouses and I draw names on Thanksgiving Day, I know just what gift I'll ask for when the question arises: what do you want for Christmas?

We have a fifty dollar limit for the one name we draw, and I've given thought and this is what I'd like: the gift of the story of Three Perfect Strangers. My request will be that whomever draws my name will, in the course of one day, spend the money on three perfect strangers, in whatever way might brighten their day: paying for lunch at a drive-thru, sending flowers anonymously, handing over a gas card or gift card for a pizza or a twenty-dollar bill. I don't know. The gifts will make themselves known to the giver, and my gift will be, when we gather at Christmas, to hear the story of those three perfect strangers and what they received and how, in the spirit of giving.

I imagine this could take some work, but no more work than choosing a material gift for me. It's rumored I'm tough to buy for, and I suppose it is, as I don't have an affinity for things, and I wear pretty much the same general outfit all the time, and I am not a jewelry person, and I tend to say "books or chocolate or wooden spoons or Ciara perfume" when the question arises. But what I want this year is that story, and the thought that three lives were lit up, if only for a few moments, in the spirit of the season, of giving gifts without attachment, without expectation, without anything but warmth of heart, and thoughtful attention. It feels a bit selfish, this request. And maybe it is. But it's number one on my short list of two things. The second thing? That's for another day. I've been invited to a cookie exchange, and I've got some baking to do.

The Sugar Cookie

1 cup butter
1 cup sugar
3 eggs
1½ tsp vanilla

3½ cups flour
2 tsp baking powder
½ tsp salt

Cream butter and sugar. Add eggs and vanilla; mix. Add remaining ingredients. Mix well. Chill dough for 3 hours or so. Roll out, as thin or thick as you wish; cut with festive cookie cutters. Bake on ungreased cookie sheets at 350-375 for ten minutes. Frost with powdered sugar frosting. See bottom of page 135 for frosting recipe.

Recipe doubles easily. You may substitute almond extract for vanilla.

Snowballs

1 cup butter
½ cup powdered sugar
1 tsp almond extract

2¼ cup flour
¼ tsp salt
¾ cup oatmeal

Cream butter with powdered sugar. Add almond extract. Stir. Add flour, salt, and oatmeal. Mix. Roll dough into balls the size of walnuts. Bake at 400 on ungreased cookie sheets for 10-12 minutes. Roll in powdered sugar when cooled a bit, then again when even cooler. Makes about 4 dozen.

Melt-in-Your-Mouth Sugar Cookies

1 cup butter
1 cup powdered sugar
1 cup white sugar
1 cup vegetable oil
2 eggs
2 tsp almond extract

4 cups + 4 heaping Ts flour
1 tsp salt
1 tsp soda
1 tsp cream of tartar
colored sugars—green, red, etc.

Cream butter and sugars until fluffy. Stir in oil, and then eggs and extract. Add dry ingredients (except colored sugars). Mix well, and chill. Roll into balls, roll in colored sugar, and flatten. Bake at 350 for 10 minutes or so. Makes about 6 dozen. Mmm.

Mrs. Sundberg's Perfectly Good Spritz

2¼ cups flour
¾ cup sugar
½ tsp salt
1 cup butter

1 egg (measure with water to ¼ cup)
1 tsp almond extract
Food coloring, optional
Cinnamon imperials, optional

Sift dry ingredients together. Cut in butter until you've got fine lumps. Add egg and vanilla, combine. Divide dough and add red, green or blue food coloring. Mix in with hands. Chill dough an hour or so, and fill press. Form cookies and decorate with cinnamon imperials. Bake at 375 on ungreased sheets, 10-12 minutes.

Chocolate Truffle Cookies

4 squares (1 oz each)
   unsweetened chocolate

2 cups semi-sweet
   chocolate chips, divided

⅓ cup butter

1 cup sugar

3 eggs

1½ tsp vanilla

½ cup flour

2 T baking cocoa

¼ tsp baking powder

¼ tsp salt

Confectioner's sugar

Melt unsweetened chocolate, 1 cup chocolate chips, and butter. Cool. Beat sugar and eggs for 2 minutes in mixing bowl. Beat in vanilla and the chocolate mixture. Combine flour, cocoa, baking powder, and salt. Beat into chocolate mixture. Stir in remaining chocolate chips. Cover and chill about 3 hours. With lightly floured hands, roll into 1 inch balls and bake on ungreased sheets at 350 for 10-12 minutes, or until lightly puffed. Cool and dust with confectioner's sugar. Makes 4 dozen cookies.

Mrs. Jungerberg's Peanut Blossoms

1 cup butter
1 cup peanut butter
1 cup white sugar
1 cup brown sugar
2 eggs

1 tsp vanilla
3½ cups flour
2 tsp baking soda
1 tsp salt
1 bag chocolate stars or kisses

Cream butters and sugars. Add eggs and vanilla; mix well. Add dry ingredients and mix gently until blended. Roll into walnut-sized balls and roll in white sugar. Place on ungreased cookie sheets and bake at 350 degrees for 8 minutes. When done, press a chocolate star or kiss in the center of each cookie, and put back into the oven for 2 minutes or so. Makes a big ol' batch.

Almond Bark Squares

24 oz almond bark
1 large box Wheat Thins crackers
1 jar creamy peanut butter
Various holiday cookie decors

In large, shallow bowl, melt almond bark in microwave according to directions. Spread peanut butter on a Wheat Thin; top with another Wheat Thin. Using a fork, dip "sandwich" in almond bark and flip over, being sure all sides are coated. Place on foiled sheet or wax paper. Sprinkle with nonpareils or festive decors. Let dry until bark is set.

White Chocolate Chippers

1 cup butter or margarine, softened
¾ cup granulated sugar
⅔ cup packed brown sugar
1 tsp vanilla
2 eggs

2¼ cups flour
⅔ cup baking cocoa
1 tsp baking soda
¼ tsp salt
1½ cups white chocolate chips

Cream butter, granulated sugar, brown sugar and vanilla extract in large mixing bowl. Add eggs and beat further. Mix in flour, cocoa, baking soda and salt. Stir in chips. Drop by teaspoonful onto ungreased baking sheets. Bake at 350 for 9 to 11 minutes.

Fattigmand

6 egg yolks
4 T sugar
1 T melted butter
⅛ tsp salt

3 cups flour
6 T sweet cream
⅛ tsp ground cardamom
Powdered sugar

Beat yolks. Add sugar and mix. Add rest of ingredients and mix well. Roll thin and cut into diamonds. Deep fry at 370 for 2-3 minutes, until golden brown. Roll in powdered sugar and serve.

Use ice water when making pie crust from scratch.

Chocolate Cherry Cookies

1 cup butter
1 cup sugar
1 cup brown sugar
1 cup oil
1 egg
1 tsp vanilla
1 tsp almond extract
3½ cups flour
1 tsp cream of tartar

1 tsp soda
1 tsp salt
1 cup oatmeal
2 cups semisweet chocolate chips
1 cup Rice Krispies
1 cup coconut
About half a jar of chopped
  maraschino cherries
Chopped walnuts, optional

Cream together butter and sugars. Stir in oil, egg, vanilla and almond extract.
Mix well. Add flour, cream of tartar, soda and salt. Mix, and add oatmeal,
chocolate chips, Rice Krispies, coconut, cherry pieces and walnuts, if you
like. Combine well. Drop by teaspoonsful onto a cookie sheet. Bake at 350 for
12-15 minutes or so. Let cool awhile.

Cranberry Macadamia Nut Cookies

1 cup butter
1½ cups brown sugar
2 eggs
1 tsp vanilla
2¼ cups flour
1 tsp soda
1 tsp salt
1 cup macadamia nuts
1 cup white chocolate chips
1½ cups sweetened, dried cranberries

Cream butter, sugar, eggs and vanilla. Add flour, soda and salt and then mix. Fold in nuts, chips and dried cranberries. Drop by spoonfuls onto cookie sheet and bake for 9-10 minutes at 375.

Christmas Eve

· · · · · · · · · · · · ·

Chipped Beef Dip

Sauerbraten Pot Roast

Creamy Baked Vegetables

Swiss Cherry Cheese Torte

Charlotte's Christmas Rice Pudding

Made rice pudding on Saturday, and it was pretty good. I'll confess I got a bit emotional a few times while I was baking. I was listening to the Prairie Home Show, and Mr. Keillor did a go-round of "Silent Night" and that always gets my throat all bound up and I can barely sing along. And then there was that whole story about the man and woman who left a party and sat in his car talking about the things they love and then he proposed to her, right there out of the blue. And she said "yes." Oh, my. There I was, tears all the heck over, trying to eat my French toast at dinner. "What's wrong, Mom?" the kids asked. It's just the Spirit of Christmas, I told them. Gets me sometimes.

The Christmas Spirit is a strange and wild thing. Things happen you can't explain, mysterious things and beautiful things, and you'd best go with the flow or you'll lose your mind. I haven't been able to fall asleep before midnight for a good ten days now. Mr. Sundberg thinks it's a bit odd. "You were doing what at 12:30 a.m.? Baking spritz cookies? Is everything okay? Maybe you need one of those spa weekends." Christmas Spirit, I told him. I'll sleep next year.

It's the Christmas Spirit, I imagine, behind the anonymous gift of $100 that came to our house on Wednesday of last week, with a note attached reading, "Enjoy something local." And behind the plates of cookies and loaves of bread on the counter from friends and neighbors. Someone shoveled our walk for us early this morning, and the Andersens put up an inflatable nativity scene, complete with a hovering angel. My mother called on Sunday—she'd accidentally doubled an already-doubled recipe and ended up with over 300 peanut blossoms. I didn't believe her when she told me she took a box of them down to the hardware store and stood with the bell ringer and handed out cookies. Until I saw the evening news.

People are eating berry compote and wearing sweaters that light up and ties that play music. They're donating hams and turkeys to the food shelf and calling their grandparents and baking cookies with their children late into the night. They're weeping at intersections and searching for the perfect gift and working longer hours. The scent of pine is everywhere. And so are bowls of chocolate, and nuts and the perplexity of fruitcake. It's Christmas, and we are not ourselves. Cheers, and a merry one to you, and to yours.

Chipped Beef Dip

8 oz cream cheese
2 T milk
1 pkg chipped beef
2 T chopped green pepper
½ cup sour cream
½ tsp onion salt (or more, if you wish)

Combine ingredients. Pour into shallow casserole or 8x8 pan. (I like to garnish this dip with a tree made of green pepper strips). Warm 15 minutes at 350. Doubles easily. Serve with Fritos.

Add 2-3 cubes chicken or beef bouillon to 1-2 cups hot water and pour in bottom of turkey, chicken or beef roaster before cooking. Adds flavor to juices and gravy.

Sauerbraten Pot Roast

4-5 lb boneless beef, chuck or top blade roast, ½ lb per person

1 large yellow onion, chopped

1 T oil

1 pint of cider vinegar

1 cup sugar

1 T whole cloves

1 T whole allspice

1 T salt

3 small hot peppers or drop of Tabasco sauce

2 bay leaves

1 quart water

¼ cup red wine

1-2 T lemon juice

¾ cup flour

½-1 cup raisins

½-1 cup raw almonds

Three to four days before serving, brown onion in oil in a 3 qt saucepan. Add vinegar, sugar, cloves, allspice, salt, peppers, bay leaves, and water. Bring to a gentle boil; cook 5 minutes; cool. Cut roast into 4-inch chunks and prick with fork. Place meat in a Ziploc bag, add marinade, seal, and refrigerate. Turn daily.

To cook, bring marinated beef to room temperature. Remove beef from marinade, pat dry and set aside. Preheat oven to 325. In a heated and oiled stove pan, brown beef on all sides, about 5 minutes each side. Place beef in oven pan. Remove bay leaves, cloves and allspice from marinade, and pour to halfway up the meat. Cover. Braise roast in oven, turning every half hour for 2 to 3 hours until tender. Reduce liquid in pan by half 30 minutes before roast is done; pour in wine and lemon juice.

For gravy, whisk flour in with the meat juices and fat in the browning pan on stove. Add remaining marinade. Cook until slightly thick. Add raisins and raw almonds before serving. Carve roast against the grain into ¾ inch thick slices and arrange on serving platter. Serve with potatoes and vegetables.

Creamy Baked Vegetables

8 oz cream cheese, softened
⅓ cup milk
¼ cup Parmesan
A couple pinches of basil
4 large carrots, sliced diagonally
8 oz fresh asparagus, cut in 1 inch segments
8 oz sugar snap peas
1 large red pepper, chopped
1 (6 oz) pkg stuffing mix (chicken flavor)

Mix together your cream cheese and milk in a large bowl, then microwave on high for about a minute until the cheese is melted. Add Parmesan and basil. Stir together, and add veggies.

Pour mixture into a greased 9x13 baking dish. Prepare stuffing according to the box instructions and scoop evenly over the veggie mixture. Bake about 30 minutes at 350. Makes a lot.

If it goes along with what you're serving, some garlic adds a nice touch to this one.

Swiss Cherry Cheese Torte

1 Swiss or dark chocolate cake mix
1 can cherry pie filling
4 oz cream cheese

2 tsp lemon juice
1 can vanilla frosting

Prepare cake mix as directed. Divide batter evenly between two 8" greased and floured round cake pans. Cool. Slice each layer into two thin layers.

Make frosting by beating cream cheese and lemon juice until smooth. Fold in vanilla frosting. Spread frosting toward outside and cherry pie filling more toward inside between layers, with frosting dripping down sides and cherries sliding off the top. Refrigerate.

Charlotte's Christmas Rice Pudding

1 qt milk
½ cup sugar
½ cup uncooked rice
½ tsp salt

½ stick cinnamon (or ½ tsp cinnamon)
½ cup cream
2 egg yolks
½ cup raisins

Put first 5 ingredients in top of double boiler, and cover. Bring to a boil, and reduce heat to medium low. Cook until rice is done, stirring often (will take a couple hours). Beat cream and egg yolks together, add to rice mixture, cover and cook another half hour. Add raisins and pour into lightly buttered serving dish. Serve warm or cold, plain or with cream.

Enjoy!

New Year's Eve

· · · · · · · · · · · · · ·

Ugly Crab Dip

Garlic Roasted Pork

Garlic Smashed Potatoes

Cheesecake, New York Style

Vodka Slushies

Made crab dip on Saturday, and it was pretty good. I was at my parents' kitchen table for most of the evening, in the midst of a large number of nieces and nephews and brothers and sisters-in-law and three dogs. It had been a happy day, and there was food everywhere—dips and cheeses and ham sandwiches and cherry pie. For a short while as I sat there, pretty much unable to move, with the nieces and nephews screaming for joy in the background, a dog shoving its head up onto my lap every few minutes, and my father offering me a chili pepper beer just to try. I felt at complete and utter peace.

It's not something you can pencil in, like a visit to the hairdresser. Real peace is elusive, and sometimes it comes out of nowhere, when you least expect it. You simply have to welcome it and enjoy it while you have it, because if your life is anything like mine, it isn't going to be around long. I tried that. Instead of making a New Year's Resolution, I pick a word I want to make more a part of my life, and I chose the word "peace" one year. I read books about it, I talked about it, I researched it, I meditated upon it. Did all I could to make "peace" a bigger part of my life. Unfortunately, that was the same year the kids got a potbellied pig for a pet, our neighbor Mr. Tully bought himself a drum set, and the garage roof was ripped off by what they say was a severe storm but what I saw with my own eyes was a small tornado. Sure, I found peace, but it came and went like the seasons themselves.

Anyway, I would recommend the whole choose-a-word-for-a-year exercise over a New Year's resolution any day. It's a manageable endeavor, and you don't set yourself up. There's really no way you can fail. And no, peace is not a major part of my daily life, but when I feel it, I recognize and appreciate it. And it does appear a bit more frequently than it once did. Same thing happened with "patience." And "tenacity." And "forgiveness."

Haven't chosen my word for this next year yet. I'm down to a short list, though. "Happiness" and "truth" and "courage" are among the choices. So are "flight" and "nutmeg" and "flexibility." I'm not worried; I'll get there. Until then, the kids have gift cards for a bookstore or two, I've a slew of decorations to box up, and I'm thinkin' sweet and sour pork and eggrolls for New Year's Eve next year. Something spicy. To kick off another Happy New Year.

Ugly Crab Dip

8 oz cream cheese
1 can crab meat, strained
1 bottle chili sauce

Place cream cheese on serving plate. Spread crab meat over and cover with chili sauce 'til it looks right. Eat with crackers.

Garlic Roasted Pork

1 boneless pork loin roast
2 cloves garlic
1 cup hot water
2 bay leaves

1 clove
2 T soy sauce
2 medium onions
Salt and pepper

Trim excess fat from roast and brown nicely over medium heat in whatever pan you prefer. Peel and thickly slice garlic cloves. Press the tip of a knife here and there into the pork and slide in a slice of garlic. Do this in proportion to how much you like garlic, with 2 cloves as the minimum. Place roast in crock pot along with a cup of water and the bay leaves, clove and soy sauce. Cover with sliced onion; add salt and pepper. Let cook in crock pot on high for an hour and on low after that. A good 4-5 hours ought to do it, depending on the size of the roast.

Garlic Smashed Potatoes

2 lbs red potatoes, quartered or halved baby reds
½ cup grated Parmesan cheese
¼ tsp steak seasoning (optional)
2-3 cloves garlic, chopped and lightly browned in olive oil
  (or use ¼ tsp garlic powder)
1 cup milk
½ cup sour cream
2 T butter
Parsley or rosemary, optional

In a medium saucepan, cover potatoes with water and bring to a boil. Reduce heat to medium and cook 10 to 15 minutes or until potatoes are tender. Drain and return potatoes to saucepan on low heat. Sprinkle with Parmesan, steak seasoning and garlic. Mash potatoes, gradually adding milk, sour cream and butter, and a bit of parsley or rosemary if you wish. Mix until potatoes are fluffy. Serve, or spoon into lightly buttered 1½-quart baking dish and cover. Keep warm in oven up to an hour and serve.

Cheesecake, New York Style

1 cup graham cracker crumbs
¾ cup sugar
¼ cup plus 2 T melted butter
1½ cup sour cream
2 eggs
2 tsp vanilla
1 lb cream cheese, broken into small pieces

Blend crumbs, ¼ cup sugar and ¼ cup melted butter. Press into bottom of 8- or 9-inch spring form pan.

Blend sour cream, ½ cup sugar, eggs and vanilla in blender, about a minute. Add cream cheese, and blend 'til smooth, and add 2 T melted butter and blend a bit more. Pour on top of crust. Bake in lower 3rd of oven at 325, about 45 minutes. Remove. Turn oven to broil, and put cake back in 'til attractive brown spots appear. Remove, let cool a bit, and refrigerate 4 hours, or overnight. Serve with cherry or blueberry topping. Serves 8-12.

Wooden spoons are good. A variety of them. And so are flour sack towels. Give old wooden spoons as gifts, as they work the best, and stitch a few words on a flour sack towel to personalize it for someone you love. Quote them, even. "Life isn't fair, and the sooner you realize it, the happier you'll be." Something like that.

Vodka Slushies

9 cups water
2 cups sugar
4 green tea bags
1 (12 oz) can orange juice concentrate
1 (12 oz) can lemonade concentrate
2 cups brandy or 2 cups vodka
7-Up or sour mix

Boil 7 cups water and 2 cups sugar until sugar is dissolved. Pour into clean container or smaller bucket or ice cream pail and set aside. Add 4 green tea bags to two cups hot water. Let sit 5 minutes. Remove bags and cool, and add to the sugar/water mixture. Next add the juice concentrates, and the brandy or vodka. Freeze and serve with 7-Up or sour mix.

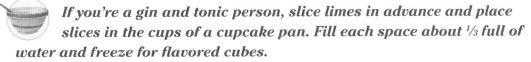 *If you're a gin and tonic person, slice limes in advance and place slices in the cups of a cupcake pan. Fill each space about ⅓ full of water and freeze for flavored cubes.*

Sledding Party

· · · · · · · · · · · ·

Garlic Breaded Chicken

Great Northern Bean Soup

Cheddar Hash Browns

Whippin' Cream Biscuits

Chocolate Cherry Cake

Made Great Northern Bean Soup on Saturday, and it was pretty good. Felt like cooking after a long day of doing things that women do. It all started with the kids whispering, "Get up! We need to get ready!" moments before the 6 a.m. alarm. It was their day with their Aunt Sue, and I was to have them in Minneapolis by noon with swimsuits and sleeping bags for a day at a water park and a night at a hotel followed by a day of sledding out at the Harke's farm. We made it with an hour to spare so I drove around awhile pretending to be lost while the kids ate the apples I'd packed for them and argued about who gets to sleep on the floor this time.

After I dropped 'em off and gave a wave goodbye, I took the long way home, stopping by several stores where I returned Christmas gifts that just didn't work out. There was a set of peach curtains from Mr. Sundberg's grandmother, curtains she thought would look lovely in the kitchen, and they would—in someone else's kitchen. We're simply not peach people, I told Mr. Sundberg and he shrugged and said, "Well, do whatcha gotta do, but I don't think they're half bad. We could use them for emergencies." Now there you go. Emergency curtains. Just in case the others fall down and we're eating breakfast naked.

So with the refund from the curtains, I bought a few rugs, since mud season is on its way, and two wooden spoons and two rubber spatulas. The good ones. If you go cheap like I did last time around, you'll be mixing along and—BOOM—the flimsy handles will snap in half and then where will you be? For nearly ten bucks a piece, these new ones ought to last a good long time. My last return was at the hardware store. Three pink flamingos, and what more is there to say. I got home earlier than I'd expected, and made myself a three-egg omelet with white cheddar cheese while I listened to the Prairie Home show. The house felt lighter, I noticed, with that pile of returns gone from the pantry. The pile on the next shelf up isn't going anywhere, though. Not for a while. Those are the gifts that are fine and lovely but could be used, well, in an emergency. You know, candles and vases and chocolates and such, anything unused, in its original package, with a reasonable shelf life. Some people call it "re-gifting." I prefer to think of them as gifts in transition. On their way from there to there, with a little stop right here. Makes sense to me. Sure does.

Garlic Breaded Chicken

1 cup crushed garlic croutons
½ cup grated Parmesan cheese
2 T flour
1 T basil
Dash or two of salt
Dash or three of pepper
4 boneless chicken half-breasts, each cut in half
1 stick butter

Mix dry ingredients together, and melt butter in a separate bowl. Dip chicken pieces in melted butter. Roll in crouton mixture. Arrange in lightly greased baking dish. Sprinkle remaining crumbs and butter over chicken. Bake uncovered at 350 for about 45 minutes. Halfway through, flip chicken over.

Great Northern Bean Soup

1½ lb chicken, cooked and chopped or shredded
2 (15-16 oz) cans Great Northern Beans, drained (or use navy beans)
1 can creamed corn
1½ T chili powder
1 T cumin
1 can Rotel chopped chilis and tomatoes
8 oz Monterey Jack cheese, cubed and added at the end

Cook for 2-3 hours on low in a soup pot on the stove, or double the recipe for a crock pot and cook on low for several hours.

Cheddar Hash Browns

1 (20 oz) pkg hash browns
1 can cream of chicken soup (cream of celery will work, too)
2 cups shredded sharp cheddar cheese
½ cup milk
¾ cup sour cream
4 T melted butter
1½ cups crushed cornflakes
¼ cup onion, optional

Mix first five ingredients well. Add 2 T butter and ¼ cup or so chopped onion (optional). Spread in a greased 2 qt glass baking dish. Mix 1½ cups crushed cornflakes and 2 T melted butter and spread over hash browns. Bake 45 minutes or so at 350.

Whippin' Cream Biscuits

2 cups self-rising flour
1 cup whipping cream

Combine flour and cream in a mixing bowl, just until blended.
The dough will be a bit stiff. Transfer to a lightly floured
surface and knead a bit. Roll to about half an inch thick and
cut with a 2 inch cutter. Place biscuits close together on a
lightly greased sheet. Bake 10 minutes at 450. Makes 12.

Chocolate Cherry Cake

Cake

1 chocolate cake mix
1 (21 oz) can cherry pie filling
2 beaten eggs
1-2 tsp almond extract

Frosting

1 cup sugar
5 T butter
1/3 cup milk
1 cup chocolate chips

Mix together the dry chocolate cake mix, cherry filling, eggs and almond
extract. Careful not to smash cherries as you mix. Pour into a greased and
floured 9x13 cake pan. Bake at 350 for 20-25 minutes or until cake is set in
middle. May also be made in a larger pan for bars.

For frosting, bring to a gentle boil sugar, butter, and milk; boil 1 minute. Remove
from heat. Add chocolate chips. Stir well. Pour over cake and let cool. Serve
plain or with whipped topping.

Football Game Get-together

· · · · · · · · · · · · ·

Hot and Spicy Cocktail Nuts

Grandpa Mike's Wings

Super Buffalo Blue Cheese Sauce

Super Bowl Dip

Beer Cheese Soup

Caramel Nut Bars

Made beer cheese soup on Saturday, and it was pretty good. I was cleaning the pantry while Mr. Sundberg spent the evening out in the garage with a number of his friends. They get together every month or so in someone's basement or garage and grill out and have a few beers or cocktails and tell jokes and stories. The weather wasn't so great, but there were seven men out there around the fire pit, and I heard a lot of laughter and they kept it going 'til after ten. Later, as we lay in bed, he told me about it. How they talked not about sports but about recent events in the news and books they have read and the people who have influenced them of late. It's his version of a Bible study, I think. Our church has one for men, but Mr. Sundberg is often out of town on Tuesday mornings early, and everyone needs a time and place to talk about the Big Thoughts.

What I found most interesting was what he said about mortality. One of his favorite writers is Tolkien, who wrote about The Gift of Men, which is mortality. "See, the Ring was the thing for the hobbits," he said. "They're mortal. Which makes them able to resist the power of the ring, and overcome it. If they lived forever, there wouldn't be anything at stake. Because they can and will die, they have to make choices." Now, Mr. S. is no Einstein, but he is well-read and up on what's going on in the world, and he's a thinker. Now and then he brings up something that gets my thoughts going. It didn't keep me up all night, but I remembered reading a good while back that Kafka said something similar, that life is meaningful because it stops.

And that's what I thought about all day Sunday while going through closets and drawers and the garage itself in preparation for the garage sale I'm putting on in the spring. I do this every few years, mostly for the conversation and because it puts the kids to work (they receive the bulk of the profits for school trips next year if they help out) and for the feeling of lightening the load of things we carry with us. If we lived forever, would we have garage sales? Would we go to yoga, or meet in garages to talk about life? Would we take such care while making a cinnamon coffeecake for a visit with a neighbor in grief?

I think I'm glad we don't live forever. That it all ends, at least here, anyway, makes washing clothes and baking a pie and getting together with each other and watching a sunset all kind of beautiful. Because everything ends. A gift, indeed, if you think about it.

Hot and Spicy Cocktail Nuts

½ cup butter
1 T Worcestershire sauce
1 T paprika
1 tsp hot pepper sauce
1 tsp salt

½ tsp garlic powder
½ tsp onion powder
¼ tsp pepper
A pinch of cayenne (or to taste)
1 pound unsalted nuts

Melt butter in a large skillet over low heat. Add the Worcestershire sauce, paprika, hot pepper sauce, salt, garlic powder, onion powder, pepper and cayenne and mix well. Add the nuts and toss well to coat. Cook for 20-25 minutes, stirring frequently over low heat until the nuts are lightly toasted. Drain on paper towels and serve hot, or store in an airtight container at room temp until ready to serve. Makes a pound of spiced nuts.

Grandpa Mike's Wings

5 lb bag frozen wings
Oil
2 sticks butter, melted

Tabasco sauce
Blue cheese sauce (page 104)
Celery sticks

Whole chicken wings come in three parts: the drumette (thickest and meatiest), the wingette or "flat," and the wing tip. To prepare, hold wing down firmly on chopping block and cut at each of the two joints from the inside out—try to get between the bones. Discard wing tips or use for soup stock. Deep fry at 375, 10 minutes for drummettes, 8 for flats. When they float, they're done. Wings can also be grilled or baked. Dredge in 2 sticks of melted butter, combined with 1-4 T Tabasco sauce. Serve with blue cheese sauce and celery sticks.

Super Buffalo Blue Cheese Sauce

1-2 tsp white wine vinegar
2 T milk
1 T finely chopped onion
1 small clove garlic, crushed
2 T minced parsley, fresh if available
½ cup real mayo

2-4 T crumbled blue cheese
   (get the good stuff)
1 T lemon juice
⅛ tsp salt
¼ tsp fresh ground black pepper
A pinch of cayenne

Mix all ingredients and serve with wings and celery sticks. Good for 2 dozen whole wings (48 pieces).

Super Bowl Dip

1 lb ground beef (or ground venison)
1 lb Velveeta cheese, cut into chunks
1 (16 oz) can diced tomatoes
   with chilies

2 tsp chili powder
1 T Worcestershire sauce
2 tsp beef bouillon

Brown ground beef and drain fat. Add all ingredients and stir until cheese melts. Serve in a crock pot with deli chips or corn chips.

Beer Cheese Soup

4 chicken bouillon cubes

3 cups water

1 can beer

1 sweet Vidalia (or any sweet onion), diced

2½ cups potatoes, raw and cubed

1 lb Velveeta cheese, cubed

2 cans cream of chicken soup

In a large saucepan, combine bouillon, water, beer, onion (I like to brown mine a bit first) and potatoes. Simmer 20 minutes, and then add cheese and soup. Simmer 30 minutes. Serve with popcorn on top.

Caramel Nut Bars

Crust

1½ cups flour

½ cup butter

¾ cup brown sugar

Topping

6 oz. butterscotch chips

½ cup white corn syrup

2 T butter

1 T water

Can of mixed nuts, cashews or peanuts

For the crust, crumble together with a pastry cutter the flour, butter and brown sugar in a greased 9x13 pan. Pat down evenly, and bake 10 minutes at 350. Cool.

For the topping, combine chips, syrup, butter and water in a saucepan and melt on low heat. Stir well. Cover crust with nuts, and evenly pour topping over. Bake 10 minutes at 350. Let cool, and cut.

Church Funeral Potluck

· · · · · · · · · · · · ·

Mrs. Sundberg's Tater Tot Hotdish

Chow Mein Hotdish

Raspberry Jell-O Salad

Cream Cheese Crescent Bars

Blueberry Streusel Bars

Made tater tot hotdish on Saturday, and it was pretty good. Had the radio on all the while, a special Prairie Home show, and it was a welcome lift for me, I'll tell you, especially with those Buddy Holly songs, and "Do You Know You Are My Sunshine?" I was singing along with that one, and the kids were wondering how the heck I knew the words. Seems to me that one goes way back to my childhood when my dad listened to the country music station while he worked making jigs down in the basement.

Funny how the words just stay with you all your life when you learn a song as a kid. Anyway, it was good to hear some happy tunes. It was a bit of a downer of a week. The weather has been somewhat crappy with rain and sleet coming down and gray skies pretty much every day. Doesn't bother me all that much, but it seems to get to people in general. It's that time of year when spirits are low for some reason. You throw the tax deadline on top of the weather, and Valentine's Day, too, and muddy driveways and salt all the heck over everything, and lack of vitamin D or whatever it is the sun gives you, and you've got yourself a good potential for bad days.

Now, I feel compelled to say something here. Last week, in my small town, a woman whom I knew only by name got so down and out that she thought the only way to make it all better was to take a gun and turn it on herself and pull the trigger and put an end to what was a lovely and productive life. And that's just what she did. Now I don't mean any disrespect to her or her life. I have experienced only mild depression, but I know that with chronic depression or mental illness, often neither medication nor the goodness of things can in some way balance it out. For some people there seems to be no way out; death seems the only option. I just don't know. I'm at a loss here. I got through it, but not everyone can. I do know that I can come up with a list of a thousand things better than dying that I might do on the worst day of my life. A good cry, for starters. A walk in the woods. An afternoon of bowling. A spending spree at the grocery store. A long-distance phone call to mom. A long letter to dad. A drive along the river. A homemade pizza. A long nap. Another good cry.

I could go on all day, but you get my drift. Instead of dying on your worst day, rent a Winnebago and head west to the Rockies. Paint your house blue. Buy a tractor and drive it around town. Do something. Be alive while you can. You might have the blues, but there's a good chance they won't last forever. Trust me on this one.

Mrs. Sundberg's Tater Tot Hotdish

1 lb ground beef
1 chopped onion, optional
2 cans of cream soup (chicken, celery or mushroom)
Salt and pepper

1 can of corn
1 can of green beans
Approximately 10 slices of American or cheddar cheese
1 bag of Tater Tots

Brown the first two ingredients and drain. Mix with one can cream soup (chicken or celery or mushroom) and spread evenly in 9x13 pan. Salt/pepper as desired. Mix 1 can corn and 1 can green beans, both drained, with a second can of cream soup. Spread over meat layer. Place layer of sliced cheddar or American cheese over vegetable layer. Arrange Tater Tots over all. Bake at 350 uncovered for 30-40 minutes.

Chow Mein Hotdish

1 lb ground beef
1 medium onion, diced
2 cups chopped celery
Butter
Salt
Pepper

1 can cream of chicken soup
1 can cream of mushroom soup
2¼ cups water
⅔ cup uncooked rice
Chow mein noodles

Brown meat, onion and celery together in pan with a little butter, salt and pepper. Combine soups, water, and rice, and add hamburger mixture, mix well. Pour into lightly greased casserole and bake at 325 for 1-1½ hours. Sprinkle with an ample amount of chow mein noodles.

Raspberry Jell-O Salad

You'll need a ring mold for this recipe.

8 oz cream cheese, softened
8 oz Cool Whip
1 cup sugar
2 (3 oz) pkg raspberry Jell-O
2 cups hot water
2 (10 oz) packages frozen raspberries

Blend together first three ingredients and pour into mold.

Dissolve Jell-O well in water, and add frozen berries. The cold berries will start to gel right away. When it begins to set, pour over top of cream mixture. Refrigerate. Unmold over lettuce. Serve with Cool Whip as topping.

Cream Cheese Crescent Bars

2 packages crescent rolls
2 (8 oz) packages cream cheese, softened
1 egg yolk (save white)
1 cup sugar
1 tsp vanilla
Cinnamon
Sugar

Heat oven to 350. Grease 9x13 cake pan. Spread one package crescent rolls flat, pressing edges up the sides of the pan just a bit. Mix cream cheese, egg yolk, sugar and vanilla. Spread over bottom crust. Lay the other package crescent roll dough over the cream cheese mixture. Seal edges.

Beat egg white with fork; smooth over the entire top. Sprinkle with cinnamon and sugar. Bake for 25-30 minutes or until light brown. Refrigerate and cut when cool.

When making bars, line pans with foil. Most bars work fine this way, and you lift 'em out when you're done. Makes cutting and clean-up a good deal easier.

Blueberry Streusel Bars

1 pkg white cake mix
½ cup softened butter
1¼ cup rolled oats
1 egg
1 can blueberry (or cherry) pie filling
¼ cup packed brown sugar

Combine cake mix, 6 T butter, 1 cup oats. Mix with a big fork until crumbly. Set aside 1 cup of mixture for topping. To the remaining crumbs add 1 egg. Mix well and press into greased 9x13 cake pan. Pour and spread pie filling over.

To reserved cup of crumbs add ¼ cup brown sugar, ¼ cup oats, 2 T butter. Mix and sprinkle over filling. Bake 30-40 minutes or until very light brown around edges.

If you wish, mix some powdered sugar, milk, and a drop of almond extract into a thick glaze. Drizzle over. Serve warm with whipped cream or chill and cut into bars.

Dinner for Two

· · · · · · · · · · ·

Bacon-Wrapped Water Chestnuts

Alaska Halibut Royale

Green Beans with Bacon

Fabulous French Silk Pie

Rum Truffles

Made some rum truffles on Saturday, and they were pretty good. It was a lovely sunlit winter day, really, and the light fall of snow we had Monday night was even lovelier, just right, the tiny sparkly flakes falling three or four flakes deep. And when the light returned on Valentine's Day, everything sparkled for a while.

Mr. Sundberg is away this week, in Nashville this time, giving a presentation about quality of life and failure to thrive and how each day ought to include laughter. Well, I agree with that one. It's Valentine's Day, year three spending it alone, and I've managed to keep my own spirits up. I got up this morning and called my neighbor Simon, 72ish, whose wife is not well and who loves a good piece of chocolate. He agreed to a road trip with me to buy a gift for his wife and we visited two local chocolateries. (I know. It's not a word, but I like it.) Though the chocolates weren't cheap, we went ahead and bought truffles and raspberry cordials and mint crèmes and something called a "Columbian Hotsy Totsy." That was the first place, and on our drive to the next we ate some chocolate with almonds and it was so good. We didn't buy much at the next apart from the colorful ten chocolates he chose for Violet, his wife. On the drive home, more chocolate was consumed and more laughter shared.

I don't know how I'll spend the rest of the day. The kids will be home soon, and there's a plate of heart-shaped cookies waiting for them. I gave each a sack of chocolate this morning, with a Valentine card and a rhyming poem I wrote myself for each. "Mine doesn't rhyme," one of them said, and when I read it aloud, I got a bit choked up.

We're having boneless pork chops with wild rice and sweet and sour sauce for dinner. I thought about shaping the pork into hearts and then rolled my eyes at myself. There will be homework, and chocolate malts and a call from Mr. Sundberg. I'll remind him how he gave me gas station roses, a handmade card, and some blaze orange underwear the first Valentine's Day we shared, and we'll laugh, long-distance, and whisper, "I love you so much."

Yes. A perfectly imperfect day. I may watch, late in the night, *Romeo and Juliet* for the 27th time. I love that story. The lesson being we really should all just get along, and that love is infinitely powerful, and that there are people out there, should we choose to seek them out, who might enliven our lives in a moment. And others, all round, who bring light to the moments in our lives. Hold them close, those people. Hold their hands. Take 'em on a road trip, or make pork for them, or dial their numbers and tell them, "I will always love you."

115

Bacon-Wrapped Water Chestnuts

½ cup soy sauce
½ cup oil
¼ cup ketchup
2 T vinegar
½ tsp pepper
4 cloves garlic, crushed
2 (8 oz) cans whole water chestnuts, drained
About a cup of brown sugar
8-10 slices bacon, cut into thirds crosswise

Mix together all but water chestnuts, bacon and brown sugar. Pour into large Ziploc bag; add chestnuts. Marinate overnight. Drain. Roll each chestnut in brown sugar, and wrap with ⅓ strip of uncooked bacon. Secure with toothpick.

Place on a broiling pan, and broil with vigilance until golden brown, turning chestnuts once or twice for evenness. Drain on paper towels. Can be prepared ahead of time and stored in refrigerator until ready to bake. For a sweeter version, simply wrap chestnuts, and baste with a mix of ¾ cup ketchup and ¾ cup brown sugar.

Alaska Halibut Royale

1 cup dry white wine
2 tsp salt
1½ lb halibut fillets
¼ cup fine dry bread crumbs
½ cup sour cream
½ cup mayo
¼ cup minced green onions
Paprika

Combine wine and salt; pour over halibut. Marinate in refrigerator for a good hour. Drain halibut on paper towel and dip each side in bread crumbs and place in shallow buttered baking dish. Combine sour cream, mayo and green onion and spread over halibut. Sprinkle with paprika. Bake at 400 for 10 minutes per inch of thickness, measured at the thickest part, or until halibut flakes when nudged with a fork. Serves 2-4, depending on how hungry people are.

To save some time, boil half a cup of wheat berries and half a cup of barley in four cups of water, along with a tablespoon of oil and a bit of salt, for half an hour. Add half a cup of brown rice and cook another half an hour or 'til tender. For flavor, try chicken or beef stock. When cool, freeze grain mixture in small containers to use with meat and vegetables and sauces.

Green Beans with Bacon

1-2 slices bacon, cooked to a crisp
1 can green beans, your favorite
⅓ cup brown sugar
1 clove garlic, chopped and lightly browned
1 tsp soy sauce
2½ T melted butter

Cook bacon and shred into small pieces, and mix with green beans (do not drain). (Reserve ¼ cup or so of the juice in case you need it later.) Mix brown sugar, garlic, soy sauce and melted butter, and pour over beans and bacon. Refrigerate overnight. Bake uncovered in a small casserole at 350 for 20 minutes or so, adding reserved juice if beans appear dry. Recipe may be easily tripled for a crowd.

Fabulous French Silk Pie

2 cups semi-sweet chocolate chips
1 cup butter
1½ cups powdered sugar
2 tsp vanilla
6 large eggs
1 10-inch baked pie crust (graham will work, too, but flour/butter is best)

Melt chips in double-boiler or microwave. Cream together butter, sugar and vanilla. Add slightly cooled chocolate. Add eggs, two at a time, beating at least three minutes after adding each pair. Pour into pie shell. Filling will be soft and piled high, but will set up in three or four hours in refrigerator.

For an 8- or 9-inch pie crust, you may cut filling recipe in half. Pie will not be as amazing to look at, but half the recipe will fill a smaller pie crust.

Serve with whipped cream, and chocolate shavings or sprinkles if desired.

Rum Truffles

2 (3 oz) packages cream cheese
12 oz chocolate chips
3 cups unsifted powdered sugar
3-4 T rum (I use 4)
2 T cocoa
½ cup powdered sugar

Combine cream cheese and chocolate chips in a bowl and microwave on high 45-60 seconds. Stir well, and microwave another 15-30 seconds as needed to melt chocolate. Mix until smooth, and add the 3 cups powdered sugar and the rum. Mix some more, cover with wrap, and refrigerate 3 hours or so. Roll into balls, and coat with a mixture of the cocoa and powdered sugar. Place on a cookie sheet covered with waxed paper and refrigerate until firm.

Sympathy Visit

· · · · · · · · · · · · ·

Three Banana Bread

Company Chicken

Mrs. Sundberg's Spaghetti Pie

Lemon Poppyseed Bread

Sour Cream Cinnamon Coffeecake

Made banana bread on Saturday, and it was pretty good. It was one of those inside days, so cold and gray outside, and I was baking when the phone call came, later in the evening. It was my mother, telling me my grandmother had died within the hour. She had lived nearly a century, and had fallen down on a Sunday in December, just after church on her way out to lunch with some friends. She never really rose up. Her hip was broken in four places, leading to pneumonia, bleeding, infection. All of it.

When she died, though, it was just right, really. A Saturday night, "Amazing Grace" playing in the background, just Grandma and her daughter—my mom—holding hands. Grandma just sighed, and was gone. Her husband died at 52; he's been waiting a long time for this elegant woman to join him. She grew up Methodist and played hymns on the organ like no one else. She gave birth to four children. She loved flowers and canning and chocolate and pie.

Mom cried on the phone. I cried, too. Not so much for my Grandmother's passing, but for myself. It's like that. Someone we love dies and we immediately want them back. I think I cried for time passing, too, and for how we each will, at some point, have said goodbye to everyone in our lives. We planned Grandma's funeral on Tuesday. There will be hymns on Saturday afternoon, and a loud organ, and purple and pink and blue flowers, and ham sandwiches and bars. I will stand up and say something, wearing one of the scarves I chose from her collection. It smells like her.

I'm not put off by the thought of my own funeral. I've always regarded it as down the road, not an event as much as one of the "next things" sometime in my 90s, if I am so blessed. I'm not so concerned with the details. I'm sure the kids will get it all right: a trampoline aisle in the church, "The Battle Hymn of the Republic," bowls of peanut butter M&Ms here and there, some poetry and some good words. Homemade pizza, perhaps, and some rice pudding. Lilies of the Valley. Laughter while reminiscing about one good life. That's what I'm thinking.

Three Banana Bread

1 stick butter	2 cups flour
1 cup sugar	1 tsp baking soda
2 eggs	½ tsp salt
1 tsp lemon juice	Dash or two of cinnamon
3 bananas	⅓ cup milk

Cream butter and sugar. Add eggs, lemon juice and bananas. Blend. Add dry ingredients and milk. Mix well. Grease and flour bottom of 9x5x3 pan. Pour batter into pan and sprinkle with sugar. Bake at 350 for 60-70 minutes. Remove from pan. Cool.

Company Chicken

4 large boneless chicken breast halves	Butter
3 beaten eggs	8 oz sliced mushrooms
1 cup seasoned bread crumbs	Sliced white cheese
	¼ cup canned chicken broth

Pat chicken dry. Pour eggs over chicken in bowl and refrigerate 1-2 hours. Drain, and dredge chicken in bread crumbs. Brown in melted butter 3-4 minutes on each side. Place in glass dish or casserole. Cook mushrooms in butter until soft. Spoon over chicken. Top with cheese and broth. Bake at 350 for 30-45 minutes.

Mrs. Sundberg's Spaghetti Pie

6-8 oz cooked spaghetti, cooled a bit
1 egg
¼ cup Parmesan cheese
Dash or two garlic salt
1 T parsley
1 cup shredded mozzarella
1 jar Prego or your favorite spaghetti sauce

Mix together pasta, egg, ¼ cup Parmesan, garlic salt and parsley. Pour into lightly greased pie plate or baking dish. Press gently from center toward edges to form a "crust."

Layer shredded mozzarella cheese over spaghetti and press down a bit.

Pour as much of a jar of your favorite spaghetti sauce over as will reasonably fit. I like Prego, myself, but I make my own on occasion. You can add ground beef, more cheese, pepperoni, or any thing else you wish. Mushrooms sautéed in olive oil, perhaps.

Bake at 350 for 25 minutes. Serves 4.

To double, use 12-16 oz cooked spaghetti (using more gives a thicker base) and 2+ cups of cheese, etc. Bake in a greased 9x13 cake pan at 350 uncovered for 35-40 minutes.

 Thaw steak or other meat in a cast iron frying pan on the stove. It'll thaw faster than sitting on the counter.

Lemon Poppyseed Bread

4 eggs
1 small instant lemon pudding
1 lemon cake mix
½ cup oil
½ cup poppy seed
1 cup water

Glaze

¼ cup sugar
1 T lemon juice

Mix all ingredients well. Pour into 2 lightly greased loaf pans, or one loaf pan and 12 muffin cups. Bake at 350 for about 45 minutes. Consider glazing with a mixture of lemon juice and sugar.

Sour Cream Cinnamon Coffeecake

½ cup butter, softened
½ cup shortening (Crisco)
1 cup sugar
2 eggs
2 cups flour
1 tsp baking soda
½ tsp salt
1 cup sour cream
1 tsp vanilla

Topping

½ cup sugar
2 tsp cinnamon
⅓ cup brown sugar
1 cup chopped pecans, optional

Cream butter, shortening and sugar. Beat in eggs. Combine flour, baking soda and salt. Add to mixture, alternating with sour cream and vanilla. Pour ½ batter in greased 9x13 cake pan. Sprinkle with ½ topping. Drop remaining batter on by spoonsful, spreading slightly. Sprinkle with remaining topping. Bake at 350 for 30 minutes or so.

Optional: add 1 cup chopped pecans to topping.

Enjoy!

A St. Patty's Day Feast

· · · · · · · · · · · · ·

Mini Reubens

Irish Brown Bread

Irish Boiled Dinner

Caramel Shortbread Bars

Pistachio Cake

Made pistachio cake on Saturday, and it was pretty good. Irish things, and green, and a jig now and then around the house. Unfortunately, I got so swept up in my taxes and rushing around that I didn't have it in me to run to the store for corned beef and rye. That's how it goes some years. You get all jacked up about a holiday, and then it's here, and you're caught unprepared. Silly. So we ended up having fried egg sandwiches, which are tied with reubens, in my mind, for Best Sandwich of All Time.

The best reuben I've had was made for me by a boy I had an eye for way back when I was a girl. We'd dated a few times and didn't know much about each other except how drawn to each other we were, and when he invited me to his home for dinner one Wednesday night before the church Lent service, I about cartwheeled. It was this time of year, and he was even more Irish than I, so the meal was his specialty. He cooked; I watched. He carefully fried the sauerkraut, then set it aside. Then he fried the corned beef—not crisp, but so it was a little brown and sweet around the edges. Then he assembled the sandwiches in the pan with the hot ingredients, some light rye without caraway seeds, and big slices of Swiss cheese. The bread came out toasted just right, and he poured, without discretion, the most wonderful Thousand Island dressing in a bowl for us to share. He even lit a candle, and we sat there, laughing, dipping our huge sandwiches in dressing while his parents watched the evening news. To this day, I've yet to enjoy a reuben as satisfying.

Fried egg sandwiches, on the other hand, rank high among the most comforting of foods. My mother made them for me on my adolescent Saturdays when the world seemed far too vast and I could not find myself. She made a fried egg sandwich when I didn't make the play, and another when my report card was substandard. She made another when the boy who made the reuben showed up with another girl at the school dance, and yet another after I worked a long hot double shift at the McDonald's drive-thru window. Two eggs, two slices of white bread, a little salt, pepper and butter—that's all. Pure comfort.

Mini Reubens

1 pkg sauerkraut
4 T relish
1 cup mayonnaise
¼ cup ketchup
1 loaf mini rye bread, sliced
1 pkg pastrami
Baby Swiss cheese, sliced

Preheat oven to 325 degrees. Prepare sauerkraut as directed. Remove from bag and squeeze out any liquid. Mix together relish, mayo and ketchup to make Thousand Island dressing and spread on bread. Assemble on baking sheet lined with tin foil. Put pastrami on the dressing-coated rye bread and top with sauerkraut and a slice of baby Swiss. Bake until cheese is melted, about 5 minutes. Remove from oven and serve.

 For a finer texture, use milk instead of water when you're baking bread.

Irish Brown Bread

    2 cups whole wheat flour
    2 cups white flour
    1 tsp salt
    1 tsp baking soda
    2 T wheat germ
    1 T butter
    2 T honey
    2¼ cups buttermilk (approx)

Mix together all dry ingredients. Rub in butter. Form a well in center and pour in honey and buttermilk; mix well. Turn out on floured board and knead lightly. Form into a round and cut across the top to prevent cracking. Put into greased and floured 8- or 9-inch cake pan and bake at 350 for 45 minutes to an hour, or until knife inserted in center comes out clean.

Irish Boiled Dinner

1 (3½ lb) fresh beef brisket

2 (12 oz) bottles lager beer

2 cups water (or enough to just cover)

2 bay leaves

10 black peppercorns

½ cup chopped fresh parsley

2 tsp salt

3 cloves garlic, peeled and sliced

2 cups chopped and rinsed leeks (white parts only)

1 medium yellow onion, peeled and sliced

2 T butter or olive oil

¾ lb large carrots, cut into large pieces

¾ lb small red potatoes

1 lb turnips, peeled and quartered

2 lb green cabbage, cut in sixths (secure with toothpicks)

Salt and freshly ground black pepper to taste

Place an 8-10 qt Dutch oven on the burner and add the beef, beer, water, bay leaves, peppercorns, parsley and salt. Heat a frying pan and saute the garlic, leeks and yellow onion for a few minutes in butter or olive oil, then add to the Dutch oven.

Cover and simmer gently for 3½ hours or until the meat is very tender. (This will take about 1 hour per lb of brisket.) In the last 25 minutes of cooking, add the carrots and red potatoes. In the last 15 minutes of cooking, add the turnips, cabbage, salt and pepper. If the vegetables are not done to your liking, cook them longer, but do not overcook. Remove toothpicks from the cabbage before serving.

Caramel Shortbread Bars

Shortbread

2 cups flour
½ cup brown sugar
½ tsp salt
¾ cup butter, chilled

Caramel

½ cup butter
½ cup brown sugar
¼ tsp salt
2 (15 oz) cans sweetened condensed milk
1 tsp vanilla

Frosting

10 oz dark or semi-sweet chocolate, chopped
4 T butter, softened

Preheat oven to 350. Line a 9x13 inch baking pan with aluminum foil and lightly grease. Combine flour, sugar, salt and butter with a pastry cutter, until it reaches a sandy consistency and the butter is mixed in. This can also be done by hand, rubbing the butter in with your fingertips. Transfer mixture to prepared pan, spread evenly and press into a firm layer. Bake for 35 minutes, until light golden brown. Cool.

To make the caramel, combine butter, brown sugar, salt and sweetened condensed milk in a medium saucepan. Cook over medium heat, stirring constantly (making sure to scrape the bottom and sides of the pan), until caramel comes to a boil. Reduce heat to medium-low and cook for 4-5 minutes while stirring until caramel thickens. Remove from heat and add vanilla. Pour caramel onto cooled crust and spread into an even layer. Cool.

*A simple variation on the caramel layer: melt 1 bag Kraft caramel bits with 2 T milk in place of above caramel ingredients. Spread over cooled shortbread, and continue.

To make the frosting, melt together chocolate and butter, stirring until mixture is very smooth. Pour onto caramel and spread into an even layer with a spatula. Cool, slice and serve. Makes about 36.

Powdered sugar frosting is easy, too. Pour a 16 oz pkg of powdered sugar into a bowl. Add a mix of 2 T melted butter, half a cup of milk and 2 tsp almond extract (optional). Stir. Add milk as you go until frosting is of the right consistency for drizzling, spreading on cookies, etc.

Pistachio Cake

1 box white cake mix
1 cup oil
1 cup 7-Up or Fresca
3 eggs
2 small boxes instant pistachio pudding
1¼ cup milk
1 tsp vanilla
8 oz Cool Whip

Whisk cake, oil, 7-Up, eggs and 1 box pudding until blended, and mix another 2 min. Bake in a greased and floured tube or 9x13 pan at 350 for 40-45 minutes.

For the frosting, mix remaining box pistachio pudding with 1¼ cups milk. Add 1 tsp vanilla and 1 (8 oz) container Cool Whip. Fold together until blended. Frost when cake is cool. Refrigerate, and serve.

Snow Day

· · · · · · · · · · · ·

Butterscotch Rolls

Sesame Beef

Sweet and Sour Pork

Napa Cabbage Salad

Frozen Lemon Dessert

Made butterscotch rolls on Saturday, and they were pretty good. I spent a good part of the evening as I listened to the radio cooking up some white chicken chili and sloppy Joes and some gooey chocolate caramel bars for Mr. Sundberg and the kids to take along to the family cabin on Sunday. The kids are on spring break and had hoped for an adventure and Mr. Sundberg had the energy for it this time around. I have a need to catch up on paperwork and bills and such, so off they went for three days in the northland.

And what do you know? The snow I've been secretly wishing for started coming down on Monday, and kept coming down for a good 18 hours. I say "secretly" because just about everyone around is commenting on how "spring is just around the corner" and updating neighbors on the progress of the lilies and the daffodils and irises—all bulbed and sprouting and reaching toward sunny, butterflied days we can't see. Still around the corner.

When it comes to seasons, spring is the quiet sister. You've got summer with its hazy stretch of laze and sun and hammocks and books, dozing on the dock, mowing lawns and diving into rivers. I love the burning colors, the wood smoke scents and the orchards of autumn, and winter's fury and wildness, snow piled high and blowing, the sharpened definition of "cozy" that comes with it, the sense of survival mode. To me, spring is a restorative walk in the park, a cool shower. There's the scent of rain, mud holes in the driveway and the ascent of spiders on the windowpanes. Spring is WormFest, hazy green fields, berries and fluffy salads with pineapple and coconut and lime.

So much freshness and clarity and green. Which is why I keep secret, most years, my late-winter wish for just one more storm. Bring it on, dark skies, and cover the house with snow. Blanket the drive so I can't get out, so I can bake and pay a few bills and dust the shelves, and putter and putz. Let me run across a documentary by chance, something on the suffragettes or black mambas or the giant squid no one ever sees. Give me a small stretch of time for a nap late in the day, and please let there be syrup in the fridge. French toast would be good as the day sifts into night. Yes, some French toast and lit candles, and a text or two, or a call even, from the children, out romping in the twilit snow on a frozen lake somewhere out there, to the north, in this land of seasons I love.

Butterscotch Rolls

1 loaf frozen bread dough (or 15 oz pkg frozen roll dough)
1 small pkg butterscotch pudding, the kind you cook, not instant
½ cup brown sugar
½ cup butter, melted
Chopped pecans, optional

Get this recipe going the night before you want to serve the rolls. Grease a bundt or bread pan and fill with walnut-size pieces of bread dough. Sprinkle dry pudding mix over, then brown sugar, then evenly pour melted butter over the whole shebang. Sprinkle with chopped pecans if desired. Cover and refrigerate overnight. Let sit on counter until double the size of how it looked before it went into the fridge. Uncover and bake at 325, 30-35 minutes.

Sesame Beef

1 lb or so lean top round or sirloin
⅓ cup sugar
⅓ cup soy sauce
⅓ cup oil, plus extra
¼ cup sesame seeds

3-4 T cornstarch, heaping
1 cup or so water
½ cup sliced baby carrots
Four servings of rice

Slice steak into thin strips, 1½-2 inches long. Place in bowl with sugar, soy sauce and oil. (You can use 2 T oil if you're watching fat content.) Marinade for a few hours or overnight.

An hour or two before dinner, toast sesame seeds and set aside. Pour meat/marinade into a skillet with 1 T oil. Cook on medium until meat is brown. Mix 3-4 heaping tablespoons cornstarch with 1 cup water. Add to meat and stir frequently. Add more cornstarch/water mixture to thicken as desired. Sauce should be brown, not pale, and have a rich strong flavor.

About 15 minutes before serving, throw a handful of baby carrots sliced in half on top of the meat. Stir in. Carrots should be more crisp than tender. Sprinkle sesame seeds over and serve on a bed of white or brown rice.

Sweet and Sour Pork

1 lb pork loin, trimmed and cut
   into 1"x½" chunks

1 cup cornstarch, or so

Marinade

2 T soy sauce

1 egg white

1 clove garlic, minced

Sweet and Sour Sauce

1½ T cornstarch

½ cup cider vinegar

¾ cup pineapple juice

3 T ketchup

1 T soy sauce

¾ cup brown sugar

Stir Fry Ingredients

1 medium onion, quartered
   and separated

1 medium carrot, julienned
   to ¼" thickness

1 bell pepper, green or red or ½ of
   each is nice, cut into 1" squares

4 oz fresh mushrooms, halved

1 (20 oz) can of chunk pineapple
   (save juice for sauce)

Prepare marinade and mix with cut up pork in Ziploc bag. Marinade in fridge for an hour or overnight. Mix occasionally by kneading.

Combine all ingredients for sauce in 1 qt saucepan. Bring to gentle boil, stirring constantly, then simmer until thickened and clear. Keep warm. Dredge pork chunks in bowl with about a cup of cornstarch in it. Deep fry in hot oil (375 degrees or so) until done through, about 5 minutes. Drain on paper towels and set aside. Deep frying may be done in a wok or in a separate deep fryer. Heat wok (or large skillet) and add 2 T oil. Stir fry onion, carrot and pepper for a minute, then add mushroom and stir fry 1-2 minutes. Add drained pineapple chunks and sweet and sour sauce. Heat through, stirring occasionally. Add meat, stir, and cook over low heat until warm. Serve over steamed or fried rice. Serves 4.

Napa Cabbage Salad

1 good head of Napa cabbage

Dressing

½ cup sugar
¼ cup vinegar
2 T soy sauce
1-2 T oil

Stir together in small saucepan. Bring to a boil; boil one minute.

Crunch Topping

2 T sesame seeds
Slivered almonds
1 pkg Ramen noodles, dry and broken up into small pieces
Sprinkles of soy sauce

Saute in lightly oiled skillet 'til lightly toasted. Sprinkle with a bit of soy sauce while cooking.

Shred cabbage thinly (about half an inch) and at a vertical angle. Place in large bowl. Pour cooled dressing over, stir well. Sprinkle with crunch topping.

 Old family dishes and casseroles and bowls don't belong hidden away. Use them. They have a purpose, and they bring back memories.

Frozen Lemon Dessert

Crumb Mixture

    2 cups graham cracker crumbs
    ⅓ cup sugar
    1 stick butter, melted

Filling

    8 oz Cool Whip, thawed
    1 can sweetened condensed milk
    1 (6 oz) can frozen lemonade concentrate

Mix first three ingredients. Set ½ cup of crumb mixture aside. Press remaining crumb mixture into an 8x8 or 11x7 pan.

Combine Cool Whip, sweetened condensed milk, and lemonade concentrate. Mix well and pour over crust. Sprinkle with remaining ½ cup crumbs. Freeze until firm.

Easily doubles using 9x13 cake pan.

Serve on hot summer evenings or after a spicy meal.

Lenten Soup Supper

. . . .

Fish Chowder

Water Buffalo Soup

Creamy Mushroom Soup

Really Good Chili

Wild Rice Soup

Made fish chowder on Saturday, and it was pretty good. A bowl of soup can be a godsend and source of real delight. There's not enough good soup in the world, I think. And light-heartedness. And there's not enough tenderness, either. I could list a hundred things of which I'd like a bit more. Chocolate, of course, and sledding expeditions, and time to lie in bed and fool around but let's not get carried away.

I'm thankful for so much it feels silly to point out what is missing, but then how might we find more of what we wish for if we don't speak it and seek it out? I'm thankful for my friends, of course, each of you, who pause in your day to pay a bit of attention to my silliness and my agonies. And those of you who love to cook and bake as I do, and indulge me in my going on about it—for you I am so grateful. For my children and their angst and hopes, for Mr. Sundberg in his diligence and love for things like flannel shirts and good crossword puzzles and speeches that inspire and peach pie. For my parents and the trail they've blazed, and my brothers and their wives and their passionate, hard-working lives, and for their children, all sparkling with what's next. For dogs. For starlight, for cinnamon, for cotton towels and for song.

Two things I wish for all of us: tenderness and light-heartedness, especially on these snowy days when emotions run high. Pause, then, and be tender with someone, and loving, and sweet. And pause again to laugh, share a meal together, feel delight.

In his essay "Experience," Emerson said:

> I am thankful for small mercies. I compared notes with one of my friends who expects everything of the universe, and is disappointed when anything is less than the best, and I found that I begin at the other extreme, expecting nothing, and am always full of thanks for moderate goods . . .

I like Ralph, but I like you all more. Let us break bread together, then, and be thankful. For soup, for each other, for the journey. Amen.

Fish Chowder

2 T butter

2 T flour

1½ cups water

1 lb fresh or thawed fish—bluegill, sunnies, perch, etc.—cut into small pieces

3 carrots, thinly sliced

3 stalks celery, thinly sliced

1 medium onion, diced

4 potatoes, washed and cubed

1 cup milk, more as desired

Salt

Pepper

Melt butter in small pot. Mix with flour and set aside. In a large pot, bring 1½ cups water to boil. Add fish and cook 'til white. Remove fish and add carrots, celery, onion, and potatoes to water. Add more water to nearly cover veggies. Cook 10 minutes, covered. Add flour and butter mixture. Stir. Add milk to bring to desired consistency. Simmer 20 minutes. Add fish, salt, pepper.

Water Buffalo Soup

1 meaty soup bone from a
water buffalo (I use a beef
soup bone, but tell my friends
it's water buffalo)

1 T butter

2 qt water

3 T barley

2 T chopped onion

1 T beef bouillon

1 T soy sauce

1 tsp Kitchen Bouquet

3 medium carrots, julienned,
chunked or sliced

1 T parsley flakes

2-3 stalks celery

1 medium potato, cubed

4-5 fresh mushrooms, sliced

½ can water chestnuts, sliced

Pepper to taste

In a 5 quart pot, brown the soup bone on both sides in 1 T butter using high heat. Add 2 qt water to cover soup bone. Cover and simmer 2 hours or so, until meat is nearly falling off the bone. At 20 minutes into simmering, add the barley and onion.

At 30 minutes into simmering, add the bouillon, soy sauce and the Kitchen Bouquet. At two hours of simmering, remove the soup bone, trim off fat and discard. Shred the meat and return to pot along with the bone. Add remaining ingredients. Simmer 20 minutes or so until vegetables reach desired doneness. Add more water and seasonings as needed.

Optional: I often add a variety of other ingredients including any combination of the following: egg noodles, bok choy, leaf spinach, spaghetti, bamboo shoots, Oriental noodles.

Serves 6-8 as a side dish, 4-6 as a meal.

Creamy Mushroom Soup

1 lb or more white mushrooms, cleaned, quartered or sliced
1 T lemon juice
1 T butter
2 T minced shallots
1 tsp dried thyme
½ bay leaf
1 tsp salt
½ tsp fresh ground pepper
2 cups heavy cream
1½ cups chicken stock
1 tsp cornstarch dissolved in 1 T water
Minced parsley, for garnish

Chop mushrooms with lemon juice. Melt butter in 4-5 qt saucepan and lightly sauté shallots on medium heat. Add mushrooms, thyme and bay leaf. Saute over moderate heat, for about 15 minutes, or until the liquid that is released from the mushrooms disappears.

Add salt, pepper, cream and chicken stock and bring to a boil. Reduce heat and simmer for 20 minutes. Add cornstarch and simmer for 10 minutes, stirring constantly. Add a few more drops of lemon juice to taste. Serves about 4. Serve sprinkled with a little parsley.

 Instant potatoes are good for thickening stew.

Really Good Chili

2 lb hamburger, browned, with fat and juice drained off

1 cup chopped onion

3 (14-16 oz) cans dark red kidney beans (drained & rinsed)

2 large cans tomato juice

1 (24 oz) can whole tomatoes or 1 quart jar of canned tomatoes

2-4 tablespoons chili powder (per taste)

1 box of macaroni

Brown and drain hamburger. Add chopped onion, drained kidney beans, tomato juice, and whole tomatoes and juice. Season to taste with chili powder. Simmer on low for several hours, stirring occasionally. Add cooked macaroni per recipe on Creamette box (if family is in agreement). Serve with crackers and homemade bread. Makes one kettle of chili.

Wild Rice Soup

3/4 cup uncooked wild rice

7-10 slices crisp crumbled bacon

1-2 cups diced cooked chicken

1 can drained mushrooms (or 8 oz fresh sliced)

1 cup half & half

4 chicken bouillon cubes

2 T butter

1 can cream of mushroom soup

4 cups water

1 cup chopped celery, if desired

Combine above ingredients in crock pot. Cook on high up to 4 hours.

Enjoy!

Bars for Bible Study

· · · · · · · · · · · ·

Grandma's Lemon Bars

Peanut Butter Brownies

Special K Bars

Seven-Layer Bars

Kit Kat Bars

Chocolate Revel Bars

Made lemon bars on Saturday, and they were pretty good. I'd had one of those days when my head just wasn't on straight and most everything I did was either poorly done or simply a waste of time. I can't explain it. I'm generally a productive person who does pretty good work, but I, for the life of me, could not accomplish much of anything. I forgot to add baking soda to the chocolate chip cookies, I washed my jeans with my multi-vitamin in the pocket—resulting in an obnoxious yellow stain on the rear which has yet to wash out—and I accidentally threw away tickets to *Cats*, to which I'm taking the kids for a birthday celebration. Suffice to say, that's just the beginning. By day's end, I'd thickened the scar tissue where I frequently bump my head on the cupboard, I managed to put dent number seven in the car, and I realized I'd forgotten to pay a bill that was already overdue. And there was more, but you get the gist.

I saw a series of photos online recently, pictures of how crappy other people's jobs can be and how you really ought to appreciate yours. One of the photos was of a man in a plastic suit with his body half-way up the rear end of an elephant. I'm not sure what he was doing in there and I don't really need to know, but I will say that I felt something like that man on Saturday, only I wasn't wearing a suit and it was my own butt my head was up. Enough said.

One of the gratifying things about life in general is that nothing lasts forever, and even a crappy day has its own twilight. By the time I got to evening, and the lemon bars, I'd been sufficiently humbled after sifting through a week's worth of garbage, something every person ought to do once in his or her lifetime. I didn't find the tickets, but I was reminded of the significant trail one person (not to mention five) can leave behind. It got me thinking about paying attention, and how I get so wound up in everything that I forget to notice what I'm doing while I'm doing it. Might have fewer scars if I slowed it down a bit. Might not have had to throw out those cookies. Then again, I did manage to see the stars at twilight, and notice how the sky to the west was three shades of purple. So I must be on my way.

Grandma's Lemon Bars

1 cup butter, softened
2 cups flour
½ cup powdered sugar
4 T flour
2 cups sugar

½ tsp baking powder
4 eggs
4 T lemon juice, freshly squeezed
Grated rind of 1 lemon
Powdered sugar, as desired

Mix first three ingredients 'til evenly crumbly. Press into a greased 9x13 pan. Bake for 15 minutes at 325.

Combine 4 T flour, 2 cups sugar and ½ tsp baking powder. Add eggs, lemon juice and grated rind. Whisk mixture until blended and pour over cooled crust. Bake 25 minutes at 350.

When cool, sprinkle with powdered sugar.

Peanut Butter Brownies

Crust

1 box (1 lb, 6.5 oz) Betty Crocker Original Supreme brownie mix
Water, vegetable oil and eggs called for on brownie mix box

Filling

½ cup butter
½ cup creamy peanut butter
2 cups powdered sugar

Topping

2 tsp milk
1 cup semisweet chocolate chips
¼ cup butter

Heat oven to 350. Grease bottom of 13x9 pan. (For easier cutting, line pan with foil, then grease foil only on bottom of pan.)

In medium bowl, stir brownie mix, pouch of chocolate syrup, water, oil and eggs until well blended. Spread in pan. Bake 28 minutes or until toothpick inserted 2 inches from side of pan comes out almost clean. Cool completely.

In medium bowl, beat filling ingredients with electric mixer on medium speed until smooth. Spread mixture evenly over base. In small microwavable bowl, microwave topping ingredients uncovered on high 30-60 seconds; stir until smooth. Cool 10 minutes; spread over filling. Refrigerate about 30 minutes or until set. Cut into 9 rows by 4 rows. Store covered in refrigerator.

The first time you try a recipe, follow it exactly. Make notes as you go, and tweak as needed second time around.

Special K Bars

1 cup light corn syrup
1 cup sugar
1 cup peanut butter
6 cups Special K cereal

6 oz chocolate chips
6 oz butterscotch chips
1-2 T peanut butter

In 2½ quart pan, bring corn syrup and sugar to a slight boil. Add 1 cup peanut butter and stir well. Remove from heat. Add cereal and spread in 9x13 greased pan.

Melt chips and peanut butter together in microwave, 2-3 minutes on medium. Check and stir occasionally until melted. Frost. Refrigerate, or cool on counter, and cut.

Seven-layer Bars

½ cup butter
1½ cups graham crackers, crushed
1 (6 oz) pkg semi-sweet
   chocolate morsels
1 (6 oz) pkg butterscotch morsels

1 (3½ oz) can flaked coconut
½ cup chopped pecans
1 (14 oz) can sweetened
   condensed milk

Preheat oven to 350 degrees. In saucepan melt butter; stir in graham crackers. Pat mixture evenly into bottom of 13x9x2 ungreased pan. Layer in order chocolate pieces, butterscotch pieces, coconut and pecans. Pour sweetened condensed milk evenly over all. Bake in 350 degree oven for 30 minutes or until done. Cool on wire rack. Cut into bars. Makes 36.

Kit Kat Bars

1½ cups white sugar
½ cup brown sugar
½ cup milk
1 cup butter
2 cups graham cracker crumbs

½ box Club crackers
⅔ cup peanut butter
½ cup chocolate chips
½ cup butterscotch chips

To make caramel, melt butter in 2½ qt saucepan. Add sugars, milk, graham cracker crumbs, and stir. Bring to a boil. Turn heat down to medium and boil for 5 minutes, stirring frequently. Remove from burner. Line a 9x13 pan with a layer of Club crackers.

Slowly pour half of the caramel over crackers in pan. Place another layer of crackers over filling until completely covered. Pour remaining caramel over second layer of crackers, and spread gently.

Melt peanut butter, chocolate chips and butterscotch chips together. Spread over bars. Cool before cutting.

Chocolate Revel Bars

1 cup butter
2 cups brown sugar, packed
2 eggs
1 T vanilla
3 cups quick oats
2½ cups flour
1 T baking soda
1 T salt

Chocolate Filling

1 (12 oz) pkg chocolate chips
1 (15 oz) can sweetened
  condensed milk
½ T salt
2 T butter
2 tsp vanilla

Cream together butter and brown sugar. Beat in eggs and vanilla. Add oats, flour, salt, baking soda and mix well. Put ⅔ cup of oatmeal mixture in a 15x10 ungreased pan (or a 9x13 pan for thicker bars).

Melt filling ingredients together adding 2 tsp vanilla. Spread chocolate filling over oat mixture, then crumble remaining ⅓ of oat mixture over filling.

Bake at 350 for 25-30 minutes.

Cream cheese frosting is good and easy. Blend a soft stick of butter, 8 oz cream cheese, and 1-2 tsp vanilla. Add 16 oz powdered sugar slowly as you mix, less for softer frosting. Add a few drops of milk to soften.

Easter Dinner

· · · · · · · · · · · · · ·

Stuffed Mushrooms

Caribbean Glaze

Ham with Rhubarb Glaze

Scalloped Potatoes the Good Ol' Way

Caramelized Carrots

Layered Pudding Dessert

Made stuffed mushrooms on Saturday, and they were pretty good. I kept leaving the kitchen to sneak a jellybean or two from the bowl on the coffee table. I had eaten all the black ones already, and white was my next target, and I noticed my daughter watching as I popped one into my mouth. "I didn't know you like jellybeans so much, Mom," she said and I replied that it is more of a nostalgia thing for me to eat them. I buy them only once a year, the full-sized sugary ones and I suppose I eat most of them. The kids aren't much interested. They have Peeps to eat, and solid chocolate rabbits. They have mini candy bars and Tootsie pops and strange, colorful little things that fizz in your mouth.

One black jellybean is all I need to transport myself back to the basement fellowship hall of the Lutheran church of my girlhood, where on Easter Sunday there was a service at sunrise, followed by a breakfast of egg bake, sausage, cheesy hash browns, cinnamon rolls, coffee and orange juice. And next to each plate in a little paper cup was a modest pile of jellybeans. My brothers and I ate them throughout the meal, and helped clean up after on the off-chance that we'd be given leftover jellybeans, which we often were.

It wasn't the meal or the service or the array of lilies round the cross or the organ playing or the pastel dresses or hats or anything in particular that made those Easter Sundays memorable. It was all of it together. Getting up early, the hunt for candy, the fight for the bathroom mirror, the walk to church, my father dozing off during the sermon, the smell of my mother's skin, the mystery of God. And then food, good food. All of it together, all of us together, the whole ball of wax. It felt comfortable and perfect and as if everything was as it should be.

Tough to recognize a moment you'll long for one day when you're in it. Sure is.

Stuffed Mushrooms

2 packages whole white mushrooms
1 pkg Jimmy Dean sausage

8 oz cream cheese
½ cup Parmesan or Romano cheese

Gently hollow out mushrooms with teaspoon, wash, and set aside. Brown sausage, breaking into crumbles. Drain excess fat. Let sausage cool a bit and mix with cream cheese in a bowl until well-blended. Stuff mixture into hollowed-out mushrooms. Bake on a foil-lined jelly roll pan at 325 for 15-20 minutes. Sprinkle Parmesan cheese on top when removed from oven.

Caribbean Glaze

16 oz can pineapple chunks, with juice
½ cup packed brown sugar
2 T cornstarch
¼ tsp ground cloves or nutmeg
⅔ cup orange juice or ½ cup orange juice plus 4 T rum

Drain pineapple chunks, reserving juice. Add water to juice if necessary to make ⅔ cup. In a small saucepan, combine brown sugar, cornstarch and cloves. Stir in pineapple and orange juice (and rum if that's the case.) Cook and stir until thickened and bubbly, then a few minutes more. Add pineapple. Spoon over cooked ham while baking or serve on the side as a condiment. Serves 12.

Ham with Rhubarb Glaze

4 lb ham, boneless and fully cooked
½ cup water
3 cups rhubarb, fresh (or 16 oz frozen cut rhubarb)
1¼ cup sugar

⅓ cup orange juice
2 tsp grated orange peel
¾ tsp dry mustard
1 cinnamon stick

Do not preheat oven. Place ham, straight from the refrigerator, on a rack in a shallow roasting pan and add ½ cup water. Insert an ovenproof meat thermometer into the thickest part of the ham. Cover the pan tightly with foil, leaving the thermometer dial exposed. Roast at 325 until thermometer registers 135 degrees, about 19-23 minutes per pound.

While the ham is cooking, combine rhubarb, sugar, orange juice, orange peel, dry mustard and cinnamon stick in a large saucepan. Bring to a boil. Reduce heat to medium and cook, uncovered, about 15 minutes, stirring occasionally. Remove cinnamon stick.

Remove aluminum foil from ham and spoon a small amount of sauce over the ham 15 minutes before end of cooking time. When thermometer registers 135 degrees, pull ham out of the oven, and allow to stand, covered, about 10 minutes, or until the thermometer registers 140. Serve remaining sauce with ham. Makes 2¼ cups sauce.

Scalloped Potatoes, the Good Ol' Way

3 T butter
2 T flour
1½ tsp salt
½ tsp pepper
3 cups milk
6 medium potatoes, pared and thinly sliced (about six cups)
2 T chopped onion

Butter a 2 qt casserole. Make a basic white sauce by melting the butter and adding the flour, salt and pepper. Stir well. Add the milk and stir over medium heat until thick. Set aside. Wash, peel, and thinly slice (width-wise) potatoes. Place half the potatoes in casserole. Cover with about half the onion and half the white sauce. Repeat layers. Cover and bake at 350, 60-70 minutes. Test with fork to make sure potatoes are almost tender. Uncover and bake another 30 minutes.

As a variation, you may wish to throw a layer of leftover cooked ham in the middle. Also consider topping with Parmesan or cheddar cheese. Serves 4 hungry people.

Caramelized Carrots

1 small sack of carrots—regular size, not mini
2-3 T butter

Salt
Pepper

Wash carrots well. Trim ends. Slice carrots into coins as thin as two nickels. Melt butter in a skillet, heat to very hot. Add carrots. Cook on high, covered, stirring frequently, about ten minutes until carrots begin to blacken along edges. Remove from heat. Add salt and pepper to taste. Serve immediately.

Layered Pudding Dessert

1½ cups flour
½ cup crushed nuts (or oatmeal)
1½ sticks softened butter
8 oz plus 3 oz cream cheese
1 cup white sugar

1 (12 oz) container Cool Whip
2 small packages instant pudding (chocolate, lemon, or pistachio)
2 cups milk, or ½ the milk required on packages (for greater thickness)

To make crust, combine first three ingredients with fork or pastry cutter until evenly mixed/crumbly. Press into 9x13 cake pan. Bake 10 minutes at 350. Combine cream cheese and sugar; add 1 cup Cool Whip and mix, reserving remainder for topping. Spread over cooled crust. Thoroughly combine dry pudding mix and milk; spread over cream cheese layer.

Spread remaining Cool Whip over pudding, as much as you'd like. You can get a 16 oz container instead of 12 oz if you're a big fan. Sprinkle with nuts if you like.

A Rainy Day

. . . .

Sour Cream Waffles

Garlic Bubble Bread

Pepperoni Pizza Hotdish

Really Fine Dough

Neapolitan Ice Cream Dessert

Made sour cream waffles on Saturday, and they were pretty good. The last week or two were pretty good, too, but they weren't great. It's the time of year when it's mostly gray out all day and evening, and when the sun does come out it does something to the snow so if you're blue-eyed like me you've got to find your sunglasses or resign to squinting in order to get around. "The doldrums" my grandmother called it. For a long time there I thought "the doldrums" were big gray buzzard-like birds who showed up on winter days. Now I know better.

I'd like to say I'm not prone to feeling down for no particular reason, but I am. The blessing is that it doesn't happen all that often, and most times I can see it coming like a thunderstorm in June. I find a few precautionary measures can sure take the edge off, so I do a lot of whistling and singing around this time of year. I made it through all of "Amazing Grace" the other day, bellering it out as if I'd lived a life of anguish, while I made dinner. I turned on the radio full blast while I was in the shower the other night and did my own little workout to the music of one "Billy Idol." And I find garnishing hotdishes and meatloaves and pizzas and oatmeal with smiley faces can be a real lift. I use whatever ingredients are in the dish itself to make the faces and sometimes I end up with a real humdinger. Last week's meatloaf resembled the

Queen of England, and the kids thought the sliced red peppers and pepperoni on the pizza hotdish looked a bit like Satan.

Unfortunately, the things I do to give myself a lift are often a source of annoyance for others. When Mr. Sundberg had some firewood delivered the other day, I thought it would be fun to stack it in the shape of his initials. Anyone flying over our house will see, clear as day, the initials "B.S." Well, he didn't take to that, and I guess I don't blame him. He's always prided himself on wood stacked with neatness and precision. The kids have about had it with my playing the Body Rockers' "I Like the Way You Move" over and over again. And I think the neighbors are glad I ran out of sparklers. I'd found a box up in the cupboard from last July with over 200 sparklers. So every evening, I've been lighting 'em up out in the yard. What amazes me is how those things stay lit, even when you run fast, through the puddles in the driveway, arms high in the air.

Sour Cream Waffles

2 eggs
1 cup sour cream
¼ cup melted butter
1 cup buttermilk
1½ cups flour

1 tsp baking powder
½ tsp salt
¾ tsp baking soda
1-3 teaspoons sugar, optional

Combine first four ingredients. Beat until smooth. Slowly add dry ingredients. Stir until well-blended. Batter will be slightly lumpy. For dessert waffles add a few teaspoons sugar. Pour batter into waffle iron and bake as you wish. Serve with butter and syrup or with a fresh fruit topping.

Garlic Bubble Bread

1 loaf frozen bread dough
2 T melted butter
1 beaten egg

½ tsp garlic powder
1 T parsley flakes
¼ tsp salt

Thaw and soften dough. Blend together all other ingredients. Cut off pieces of dough the size of a walnut and dip into butter mixture. Place in a greased bread loaf pan until all dough is used. Cover and let rise until double in size. Bake 30 minutes at 375. Brush with melted butter. Break off chunks when eating.

 Five or six 9x13 casseroles will serve about 100 people if there's other food served. This may come in handy one day; you never do know.

Pepperoni Pizza Hotdish

5 cups cooked penne pasta (1 box)

1 (26 oz) jar of your favorite spaghetti sauce (I use Prego ricotta Parmesan)

1 (14 oz) jar of your favorite pizza sauce

½ cup Parmesan cheese

12-16 oz shredded mozzarella cheese

Sliced pepperoni

Garlic salt, oregano, basil, optional

Mix first four items in lightly olive-oiled 9x13 pan. Sprinkle with about a cup of mozzarella and about a dozen pepperoni slices cut in half. Mix again. Pat down evenly. Cover with remaining mozzarella, 8-12 pepperoni, and sprinkle with garlic salt, oregano, and basil as you wish.

Bake at 375 uncovered for about 20 minutes.

Really Fine Dough

1½ T yeast

1¼ T salt

3 cups of the hottest tap water

6½ cups flour

Mix salt and yeast with water. Pour into flour and mix until uniform, and let rise. Keep in covered container in fridge and use as needed. Half the dough makes a large pizza, 11x17 pan. Good for mini-pizzas and breadsticks, too. Keeps for several weeks.

Neapolitan Ice Cream Dessert

2 cups crushed graham crackers
⅓ cup sugar
½ cup melted butter
3 bananas, sliced in ½ inch slices (optional)
1 rectangle Neapolitan ice cream
1 cup peanuts

5 T butter
1 cup sugar
⅓ cup milk
1 cup chocolate chips
8 oz Cool Whip

Mix first three ingredients. Reserve ½ cup crumbs and press the rest into a 9x13 pan. Layer banana over crust, sliced about ½ inch thick.

Cut 1 inch slices from the block of Neapolitan ice cream; press onto bananas/crust until covered. Use all the ice cream by filling in the gaps. Sprinkle with peanuts. Place in freezer.

Melt butter, sugar, and milk together and boil for one minute. Remove from heat and add a cup or so of chocolate chips. Stir until chips have melted.

Remove pan from freezer. Spread chocolate mixture over and return to freezer for 10 minutes or so. Then take it out and cover it with Cool Whip, and sprinkle reserved crumbs over the top. Return pan once again to the freezer and leave it there for a good stretch of hours or overnight.

Let sit out a few minutes before you cut it. Serves 12.

Enjoy!

Spring Brunch

Homemade Fruit Pizza

Baked Egg Dish

Cream Cheese Coffeecake

Chocolate Éclair Dessert

Cherry Pineapple Fluff

Made cream cheese coffeecake on Saturday, and it was pretty good. First time I slowed down all week, I think, and a blessed thing that was. I don't know about you and yours, but in this house May is always a month when one seeks clarity and perspective in order to maintain a sense of sanity. With three kids wrapping up the school year, there are enough plays and award ceremonies and ball games and field trips and registrations and sack lunches and goodbyes to launch one into orbit.

I took off for a bookstore on Sunday afternoon just to get away from it all. Mr. Sundberg was on day three of a four-day break, and it was raining, and the kids were all-too-happy to head to the movie theater with him and then back home to finalize class projects and gaze out the windows at the rain. Little did they or I know that perspective was on its way in the form of a brutal tornado which, somewhere around 5:30 Sunday afternoon, reached down from the sky and—in thirty-some seconds—destroyed over 50 homes and caused the evacuation of between 350 and 400 homes in a little Minnesota town not far from ours. Injured people, too, and it set relatives to searching for people not accounted for.

Funny creatures, humans are. We get so caught up in the small and simple challenges we often choose to see as stumbling blocks rather than stepping stones. We forget to pick up the milk. The car needs new brake pads. There's not a rabbit costume to be found and the play is next week. Can't get in at the dentist until the end of the month, and where on earth did the umbrellas disappear to? We had three, for God's sake. And why is the dryer making that thumping sound?

It's a bit embarrassing when you think about it. How the world throws ordinary life at you and instead of gathering it up you let it smack you upside the head. That's why it's good to look out your window now and then. There's a lot to see. Cyclones and earthquakes, a shortage of clean water here and not enough blankets there. Strange strains of the flu and shark attacks and not enough rice to go 'round and a neighborhood wiped out in seconds. Perspective is what it is, and a boatload of it.

Homemade Fruit Pizza

Crust

½ cup butter, softened
¾ cup white sugar
1 egg
1¼ cups all-purpose flour
1 tsp cream of tartar
½ tsp baking soda
¼ tsp salt

Filling

1 (8 oz) package cream cheese
½ cup white sugar
2 teaspoons vanilla extract
Fresh strawberries, bananas, raspberries, blueberries and kiwi

In a large bowl, cream together the butter and ¾ cup sugar until smooth. Mix in egg. Combine the flour, cream of tartar, baking soda and salt; stir into the creamed mixture until just blended. Press dough into an ungreased round pizza pan.

Bake at 350 for 8 to 10 minutes, or until lightly browned. Cool.

In a large bowl, beat cream cheese with ½ cup sugar and vanilla until light. Spread on cooled crust. Arrange desired fruit on top of filling, then chill.

Baked Egg Dish

3 cups seasoned croutons

1 pkg Jimmy Dean sausage, cooked and cut up (or 1-2 cups of your favorite cooked sausage)

8 oz shredded cheddar cheese

4 eggs

1 tsp mustard (wet or dry)

1½ cups milk

1 can cream of mushroom soup plus ½ cup milk

Layer in 9x13 greased pan: croutons, then sausage, then cheese. Mix egg, mustard and 1½ cups milk and pour over. Cover with foil and chill overnight. In the morning, mix soup and ½ cup milk and pour over. Bake uncovered at 350 degrees for one hour.

Cream Cheese Coffeecake

1 loaf frozen white bread dough, thawed

8 oz cream cheese
½ cup sugar
1 egg
1 tsp vanilla

6 T butter
½ cup sugar
¾ cup flour

1 cup powdered sugar
2-3 drops vanilla
2-3 T milk, to desired consistency

Let dough rise until nearly double. Press into a greased pizza pan or a 9x13 cake pan and poke several times with a fork. Combine cream cheese and sugar; add egg and vanilla. Pour and spread over dough. With pastry cutter, combine butter, sugar and flour together until crumbly, and sprinkle over the cream cheese mixture. Let rise ten minutes, and bake at 375 for 25-30 minutes.

For topping, mix powdered sugar, vanilla, and milk (several tablespoons) to desired consistency and drizzle over.

Chocolate Éclair Dessert

1 stick butter
1 cup water
1 cup flour
4 eggs
2 cups milk
6 oz French Vanilla Instant Pudding
8 oz cream cheese
12 oz Cool Whip
⅓ cup chocolate chips
1 T butter
2 T water
¼ cup powdered sugar

Bring butter and water to a boil in a 2½ qt pan. Remove from heat. Add flour while hot, and stir well. Add 4 eggs, one at a time. Beat well after adding each egg. Spread on a greased jelly roll pan. Bake at 400 for 30 minutes. Cool.

Blend milk and pudding mix well. Add cream cheese and blend until thick and smooth. Spread over cooled crust. Spread Cool Whip over pudding.

Melt chips, butter, water and powdered sugar together over low heat, stir well, and cool a bit. Drizzle over Cool Whip. Refrigerate and serve up to 12.

Rinse pan in hot water when you're scalding milk, and the milk won't scorch.

Cherry Pineapple Fluff

1 (20 oz) can crushed pineapple, drained
1 can sweetened condensed milk
12 oz Cool Whip
1 can cherry pie filling
Miniature marshmallows (to taste)
Chopped nuts, optional

Mix together and refrigerate. Serve chilled, with sandwiches, or as a dessert.

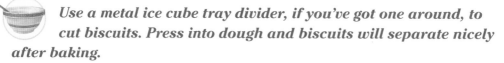

Use a metal ice cube tray divider, if you've got one around, to cut biscuits. Press into dough and biscuits will separate nicely after baking.

Mother's Day Luncheon

. . . .

Fresh Fruit Dip

Sisters' Strawberry Romaine Salad

Virginia's Almond Chicken Casserole

Amaretto Brownies

Erica's German Tea Bread

Made almond chicken casserole on Saturday, and it was pretty good. Heard a song on the radio while I was cooking, "Good Things," by the BoDeans. Oh, gosh, I love that song. I was singing it on the way out to the bus stop Monday morning. "Sunlight fall down on the fields / Sunlight fall down over me / Work all day, be all that I can be . . ." I guess I was singing a bit loud because the kids shushed me. "Mom, the bus is coming. Knock it off."

Well, how do you like those beans. Sunday was Mother's Day and they were all lovey and helped with some housework and made a fine strawberry cake for me, with sour cream frosting and a big ol' heart made with those little red-hots. They made cards, too, and gave me a pile of gifts—chocolates, a bottle of wine, some handmade almond soap and a set of three fancy knives for cutting meat. (Still no bubble machine, but there's always my birthday.) I felt a bit of mother-guilt when I took off to indulge myself in a few hours at the bookstore before we all went out for pizza and cheesecake and drove home as the sun set behind us and the frogs came out to sing. Such a perfect day.

So on Monday morning at the bus stop I was a bit surprised when they asked me to go back into the house before the bus came. "We're big enough to wait by ourselves . . . and sometimes you embarrass us." Well, how do you like that? I've nearly spent myself some mornings entertaining those kids at the bus stop. Re-enacting the first Olympics using sticks for javelins and showing them cheers from my days as captain of the cheerleading squad. Singing "Yes, Sir, That's My Baby" (choreography included), which won my high school show choir a first at state. Doing the Moonwalk as the bus pulled away last Thursday was probably the last straw, and now that I think about it I suppose I did get a bit carried away on occasion, pretending I was Daniel Boone hiding in the bushes then coming out in my coonskin cap, waving a white surrender flag before the bus. Though I think bringing hot cinnamon rolls to everyone on the bus was a nice thing because not everyone has time for a warm breakfast. And bringing coffee to the bus driver? Maybe I didn't need to go all out with the stewardess uniform, and the sparklers on the final day of school last year were probably a bit much. So, to everything a season.

I'll walk them out one last time tomorrow. I'll be good. I'll stand there and we'll talk about their day, and I'll make my way back to the house once the bus comes into sight. And when I do sing, I'll sing quietly. "You are my sunshine / My only sunshine / You make me happy / When skies are gray / You'll never know, Dears / How much I love you..."

Fresh Fruit Dip

1 (8 oz) container cream cheese
1 (16 oz) jar marshmallow fluff
Juice from one orange, optional
Fresh fruit (apples, pineapple, bananas, peaches)

Soften cream cheese, and cream together with marshmallow fluff. Try adding the juice of one orange for a tang, or using strawberry cream cheese for variety. Serve with apples, pineapple, bananas, peaches, cut and carved.

Sisters' Strawberry Romaine Salad

Dressing

½ cup mayo (light works)
⅓ cup sugar
¼ cup milk

2 T vinegar
1 T poppy seeds

Salad

Romaine lettuce, cleaned and cut, enough for everyone
A batch of strawberries, rinsed, tops removed, sliced
One lovely red onion, sliced

Mix mayo, sugar, milk, vinegar and poppy seeds together for dressing. Arrange strawberries and onion over lettuce in a bowl. Drizzle dressing over. Serve with fresh bread for a light lunch, or alongside grilled chicken or brats or just about anything.

Virginia's Almond Chicken Casserole

Casserole

5 cups diced, cooked chicken

2 cups diced celery

3 cups cooked rice

1 (8 oz) can sliced water chestnuts

2 (10.75 oz) cans cream of chicken soup

½ cup sour cream

½ cup mayonnaise

2 T chopped onion

2 T lemon juice

1 tsp salt

½ tsp garlic powder

¾ tsp pepper

Topping

½ cup sliced almonds

3 cups crushed corn flakes

⅔ cup butter, melted

Combine in a large bowl all ingredients except almonds, corn flakes, and butter. Stir well and pour into a lightly greased roasting pan, larger than 9 x 13 pan. For topping, combine remaining ingredients and sprinkle over. Bake 35 to 45 minutes at 350.

Many recipes (hotdishes, side dishes, salads, etc.) can be made in the pan or bowl they're cooked or served in.

Amaretto Brownies

Brownies

1 stick butter
2 squares unsweetened chocolate
2 eggs
1 cup sugar
½ cup flour
¼ tsp salt
1 tsp vanilla
6 oz choc chips
4 T Amaretto

White Frosting

1 stick butter
2 cups powdered sugar
1 tsp vanilla
Milk, 1-2 T or more for
    desired consistency

Glaze

1 square unsweetened chocolate
1 T butter

Melt butter and chocolate. Beat eggs until light. Beat in sugar until thick. Add chocolate mixture, flour, and salt. Stir in vanilla and chips. Bake in 8x8 greased pan at 375 for 15 min. With fork, poke holes in brownies. Pour Amaretto over. Cool.

For the frosting, blend butter, powdered sugar, vanilla and milk. Spread over brownies. Refrigerate. For the glaze, melt 1 square unsweetened chocolate and 1 T butter together, and drizzle over.

To double, use a 9x13 cake pan, and double the brownie and glaze recipes, but make only 1½ times the frosting recipe.

Erica's German Tea Bread

2 packages (2 T) dry yeast
½ cup warm water
4½ cups flour
4 T sugar
2 tsp salt
1 cup butter
½ cup evaporated milk
2 eggs

½ cup butter
1 cup packed brown sugar
1 cup chopped walnuts
1 tsp almond extract

Soften yeast in warm water, and set aside. In large bowl, combine flour, sugar, and salt. Cut in 1 cup butter until uniformly crumbly. Add evaporated milk, the yeast mixture and 2 unbeaten eggs. Mix well and chill 2 hours or overnight. Be careful not to overmix.

When ready to bake, melt ½ cup butter, brown sugar and walnuts together in a skillet. Add almond extract and leave on low heat.

Divide dough into four sections. Pat out each section to 8 inches round on a floured surface. Put 2 T (I use a bit more) of nut mixture on ½ of the round. Fold dough over into a crescent and seal. Place on a greased cookie sheet. Make cuts 1 inch apart along the outside edge and gently turn cut sections onto their sides so filling is somewhat exposed. Let rise 45 minutes. Bake at 350 for 20-25 minutes. Frost while warm with powdered sugar frosting.

Enjoy!

Graduation Buffet in the Garage

. . . .

Dad's Good Time Hot Beefs

Potato Salad

Hot Five Bean Salad (Five Beaner)

Those Chocolate Caramel Bars

Rootbeer Float Cake

Made potato salad on Saturday, and it was pretty good. Just about all of it got eaten during the big open house for our daughter. It was a four-hour event, but the build-up went for weeks and though the clean-up didn't take long, it seemed like a lot in one day. We had, at one point, over 50 people in our two-car garage, where we'd set up tables for food and gifts and eating. The rain did not hold off and it came pouring down several times that afternoon, and what can you do? You seek shelter, and hold on to your cup, and let go of your thoughts of The Perfect Day.

Some people spend years preparing for the Graduation Open House—landscaping and deck building and cultivating and so on—but we've never been much for that. Mr. Sundberg mowed and cleaned the garage and swept the drive, and I gave the house a once-over with a dusting cloth and vacuum, but beyond that we didn't do a lot. So when the rain came pouring down it wasn't a major let-down, rather a demand for small adjustments like moving tables inside and making sure the crepe paper stayed in the rafters where it wouldn't be dragged through water on the wet garage floor.

What makes a gathering good and successful isn't about the weather. It's the mix of people and the camaraderie, and if there's good food and drink on the side, that's a real bonus. We had a lovely table of hot beefs and beans and rootbeer float cake, several coolers full of pop and beer, and a modest box of rather cheap wine. There were plastic lime, pink and orange tablecloths (our daughter's color selection) and a bakery cake you could use as a weapon, it was so large and dense. And delicious. Vanilla, with raspberry filling.

And we had family there, and friends, and people from church and town and school whom our daughter invited because they've meant something to her life, and the mix of people in all of their humanness and brokenness and joy was something to behold. There was room for tension here and there, and not everyone knew everyone else, but when you get a bunch of people together in celebration, something happens. It's magical, maybe, or holy, or just my imagination, but good rises up and we raise our plastic cups to life and to onward and to the rain pouring down.

Dad's Good Time Hot Beefs

1 onion
2 beef bouillon cubes
1 large cut of beef for roasting
1 can of your favorite beer

Salt
Pepper
Ketchup, 1-1½ cups or so
Cornstarch, optional

Slice an onion and throw about half into a crock pot along with 2 beef bouillon cubes. Add 1 beef roast, cut into several chunks if it's a thick one. Place the remaining onion on top. Pour half a can of beer over the meat, salt and pepper it, and pour on about ½ cup of ketchup. Add more ketchup as time passes, up to a cup, if you wish.

Cook 8 hours on medium. Shred meat and combine with beer/ketchup marinade to desired consistency. You may wish to whisk in some cornstarch to marinade before mixing with beef, to thicken a bit. Serve on buns or dense white bread. Mmm.

Potato Salad

5 cups sliced or cubed cooked
    potatoes
2 tsp sugar
2 tsp vinegar
¾-1 cup chopped onion

1½ cup mayonnaise
Salt, to taste
Celery seed, to taste
4 hard-cooked eggs, sliced

Sprinkle potatoes with sugar and vinegar. Stir in remaining ingredients, and toss, saving eggs for last. Fold in eggs and chill. Serves eight or so.

Hot Five Bean Salad (Five Beaner)

½ lb bacon

1 lb ground beef

1 cup chopped onion

16 oz. butter beans

16 oz. Lima beans

1 can pork and beans

1 can dark red kidney beans

1 can pinto beans

½ cup ketchup

½ cup brown sugar

2 tsp vinegar

2 tsp mustard

Crisp bacon, and set aside. Brown beef and onion in the same pan. Skim off fat, and place in crock pot. Drain all beans except the pork and beans and pour into crock pot. Add ketchup, brown sugar, vinegar, mustard and bacon. Cook at high setting for 45 min; turn to low and let cook for 2-3 hours or until serving time.

Those Chocolate Caramel Bars

1 package light caramels (about 32)

⅓ cup evaporated milk

1 package German chocolate
   cake mix

½ cup butter, melted

⅓ cup evaporated milk

1 cup chocolate chips

Combine caramels and ⅓ cup evaporated milk, and cook over low heat until melted. Set aside. In large mixing bowl, combine cake mix, butter, and ⅓ cup evaporated milk. Mix with your hands until dough is together. Pat half of dough into greased and floured 9x13 pan. Reserve rest for top. Bake at 350 for 7 minutes. Sprinkle chocolate chips over crust. Pour caramel mixture over chips. Drop rest of batter over caramel mixture. Return to oven for 15-20 minutes at 350. Cool, and cut.

Rootbeer Float Cake

Cake

1 box yellow cake mix
3 oz instant vanilla pudding
2 eggs
12 oz rootbeer (A&W works for me)
1 tsp rootbeer extract

Frosting

8 oz Cool Whip
1 stick melted butter
1 cup powdered sugar
1 tsp rootbeer extract

Combine dry cake mix, dry pudding mix, eggs, rootbeer, and extract. Mix well. Bake at 350 in a 9x13 greased cake pan, 25-30 min or until firm.

Combine the four frosting ingredients and stir well. When cake is completely cool, frost and refrigerate.

You can make Orange Dreamsicle cake by substituting orange soda for the rootbeer and orange extract for the rootbeer extract.

Never go to bed with dirty dishes in the sink. For about seven reasons. Rodents and how you'll feel better when you wake up are two of them. And it just makes sense.

Father's Day Cookout

Blue Cheese Bacon Dip

Grilled Salmon

Grandpa's Beef Kabobs

Grilled Asparagus

Strawberry Shortcake

Peach Sauce

Made blue cheese bacon dip on Saturday, and it was pretty good. The skies were a bit dark just after lunch, and I kept checking to see if there was rain coming down. There isn't much as thrilling as an impending storm. All kinds of possibilities. We may lose power, have to play card games by candlelight and have a camp-out in the living room. We may have to batten down the hatches, and it could go on all night. Or, it may simply rain, hard, a little thunder here and there, rain pouring down in buckets, the kind you want to go out and stand in, dance in, even. Run through, as if you've come undone, or broken free, or lost yourself to joy.

Which is exactly what Mr. Sundberg thought happened during Sunday afternoon's storm when he turned into the driveway and found me dancing around under the eaves, rainwater gushing in torrents over me and my new blue bathing suit. I waved to him as he pulled up. He came out under an umbrella and stood there a moment shaking his head, rain spotting his khaki pants. "I thought you were going grocery shopping this afternoon," he said. I'll do that tomorrow, I told him. Just wasn't up to it. "Well, may I ask what you are doing?" he said. It's what I'm not doing. I'm not feeling crabby because there's no sun today. No, Siree. And I wouldn't be wearing this suit, either, except Mr. Johnson down the street has been at his window for a good hour now. I know his eyes are bad, but who knows how bad, and I wouldn't want to risk an unplanned visit to my friends over at the county jail.

Mr. Sundberg went up the steps into the house shaking his head. On rare occasions, I imagine he wishes he'd married someone a bit less, well, whatever it is that I am. Which is fine with me. I've never aspired to perfection where Wifehood is concerned. Perfection is reserved for very few things—air temperature, clean windows, and pie crust among them.

I could have married someone else, too. Someone who might write poems on birch bark and bring me tea in bed. But they could be allergic to cinnamon and have an aversion to garage sales and auctions, and think it silly to fall asleep holding hands. Then where would I be?

I say, bathing suit or no, get out there and dance in the rain. Someone will love you, if someone doesn't already. And if someone already does, they'll either overlook it, or come on out and join you, and wouldn't that be something.

Blue Cheese Bacon Dip

2 (8 oz) packages cream cheese

12 oz sour cream

2 (4 oz) packages of Treasure Cave blue cheese (or your favorite)

1 T balsamic vinegar

8 strips bacon (I prefer smoked)

2 T freshly minced garlic

3 T extra virgin olive oil

1 T fresh ground black pepper

Bacon grease and cracklins from the bottom of the pan

8 sprigs fresh thyme

Mix cream cheese, sour cream, blue cheese and balsamic vinegar with a hand mixer. Cut bacon into ¼ inch strips and cook to medium-well/crisp. Remove from pan. Add garlic, olive oil, and black pepper to pan without removing bacon grease. Lightly brown garlic. Scrape pan well into the cream cheese mixture and combine. Add thyme. Chill, and serve with a loaf of sourdough, crackers, whatever you please.

Grilled Salmon

1½ lb salmon

Marinade

⅓ cup soy sauce

⅓ cup brown sugar

¼ cup olive oil

Place salmon in Ziploc bag and pour marinade into the bag. Refrigerate overnight. Brush olive oil on grill. Grill salmon 6-8 minutes each side.

Grandpa's Beef Kabobs

½ bottle Kraft Zesty Italian dressing

1 T barbecue sauce

1-2 lb sirloin steak (or venison) cut into 1-1½ inch chunks, the larger, the more tender

1 large onion

1 green pepper

1 red pepper

8 oz baby bella mushrooms

1 zucchini

1 can whole cooked potatoes

Cherry tomatoes

Mix dressing and barbecue sauce together and place with meat in large Ziploc bag, and marinate 3 hours or overnight.

Alternate beef on skewers with chunks of onion, red and green peppers, mushrooms, zucchini, canned whole cooked potatoes, cherry tomatoes. Grill 'til brown on one side. Turn. Baste with marinade.

Grilled Asparagus

Take a bunch of fresh asparagus. Wash the stalks and trim the cut ends. Soak in olive oil for a few minutes. (Any olive oil will do; it doesn't have to be from a specific region of Italy.) Turn the gas grill on to med/high or prep the charcoal grill so the coals are red hot and ready to go. Lay asparagus stalks down on grill and salt and pepper quite liberally. Cover. Let cook five minutes or so, then roll stalks and cook another five or so. It won't take long; you'll have to keep an eye on 'em, and you'll know when they're done. Remove from grill. You may wish to squeeze a bit of fresh lemon over the stalks, especially if you're serving them with fish. Or make a lot, and serve as its own meal with some homemade Hollandaise.

Strawberry Shortcake

2⅓ cups Bisquick baking mix
3 T butter, melted
½ cup milk
3 T sugar
Pinch of nutmeg
Fresh strawberries sliced and sprinkled with sugar or blueberries, heated
 with 1-2 T sugar for topping

Heat oven to 425. Stir baking mix, melted butter, milk, and 3 T sugar in a mixing bowl until soft dough forms. Add a dash of nutmeg if you're a nutmeg person. Drop by 6 or 8 spoonsful on to a greased cookie sheet. Sprinkle with a bit of sugar. Bake 9-10 minutes or until light brown.

Makes 6 larger biscuits or 8 smaller. Serve with strawberries or blueberry topping. Include whipped topping for a complete meltdown.

If you're a bit tired of berries, try making the peach sauce below.

Peach Sauce

Slice 2-3 peaches, and add sugar until they're a bit syrupy. Flavor with Grand Marnier, and serve with shortcake, pound cake, lemon cake, or other light cake.

Enjoy!

Fourth of July Picnic

· · · · · · · · · · · · · · · · ·

Spinach Dip

Bun Burgers

Ham Spread

Some Really Fine Broccoli Salad

Cream Cheese-Filled Cupcakes

Watermelon

Made bun burgers on Saturday, and they were pretty good. Got me all nostalgic about summer when I was a kid, and how things were different then, and simpler, and how my brothers and I often wish for one summer day, just one, to be kids again, together.

There weren't computers back then, at least not in our house. There was a TV, but it had a 13-inch screen and no cable, so there was "Gilligan's Island" and "Tom and Jerry" and "The Brady Bunch." We didn't watch much TV, and when we did, it was something of an event. The one show we rarely missed was "Night Stalker." We'd come running in from an afternoon of swimming and take a quick shower while Dad made popcorn or chocolate malts and we'd pile on the couch all sunburned and worn out and, for an hour, have our pants scared off.

Apart from that, we mostly played outside. We rode our bikes out to "D" bridge and waded and poked dead fish with sticks and lay on towels in the sand and ate the Cheetos and licorice Mom sent along with us. We drank sugar pop and jumped from the bridge on days when the river swelled up with water from thunderstorms, and we stayed as long as we could, often biking home as the sun set. There were hot days when we set up fans in the living room and read books and dozed off, and there were days where we walked around town with pockets full of change and ate ice cream and cheese curds and played Pac Man at the cafe. We set up the tent and slept outside now and then, and kept each other awake with stories about ol' Green Eyes, who drowned in the river. Our feet were bare and our shoulders were freckled and we didn't give much thought to why we never caught any fish in Hollicker's Creek.

There's been a stretch of perfect days lately, hot, but not too hot and sunny, with a cool breeze coming through in the afternoon, and it's been pure joy watching the kids just be kids. They've been fishing down at the river several times already, and out flying kites, and they've gone through two boxes of popsicles just this past week. I want to take them sailing, but I don't have a sailboat, so the old fishing boat will have to do. Not that they mind. They just want to be out there on the water, waves lapping at the boat, dangling their fingers or feet for small fish to nibble. I'll pack some sandwiches, and some cupcakes, and Orange Crush and oatmeal cookies and green grapes. A lot like a lunch I once shared with two boys on a beach near a river in July.

Spinach Dip

1 pkg vegetable dip/soup mix (I use Knorr)
1 cup sour cream
1 cup mayo
3 small green onions
10 oz frozen, chopped spinach—thawed, rinsed, drained and squeezed
1 round loaf of rye bread, unsliced

Combine above ingredients. Mix well. Chill 3 hours. Cut out center of an unsliced loaf of rye bread and fill with dip. Or simply cut bread into chunks, or bring it along whole and shred as you eat. Good also with carrots, celery, crackers and so on.

Bun Burgers

1 can tuna or 1 can ham (grinding up Spam works great)
4 hard-boiled eggs
1 cup chopped Velveeta
3 T chopped onion
2 T sweet relish
½-1 small jar stuffed olives
½ cup mayo

Chop everything and mix in mayo. Spread in hamburger or hot dog buns, wrap in foil, and heat about 10 minutes at 250 or so.

Ham Spread

1 large can deviled ham
2 T mayo
8 oz cream cheese
Grated onion or onion salt

Mix above ingredients. Spread on bagels, buns, bread, crackers, etc.

Some Really Fine Broccoli Salad

Salad

5 cups broccoli
1 cup each: sunflower seeds, craisins (dried cranberries),
   shredded cheddar cheese, fried bacon crumbles

Dressing

1 cup Miracle Whip
¼ cup sugar
½ tsp salt
¼ tsp pepper
2 T red wine vinegar

Mix the broccoli and all of the other salad ingredients. Mix dressing. Add dressing just before serving salad. Mix well. A meal on its own.

Cream Cheese-Filled Cupcakes

8 oz cream cheese
⅓ cup sugar
1 egg

6 oz chocolate chips
Dash salt
1 box chocolate cake mix

Combine cream cheese and sugar; mix in egg, then chips and salt.

Make your favorite chocolate cake mix according to directions. Fill muffin cups half full of batter, drop a healthy teaspoonful of cream cheese filling into center, add a bit more batter 'til cream cheese is covered and muffin cup is about ¾ full. Follow directions on cake mix box for baking cupcakes.

Watermelon

1 large, ripe watermelon
1 large, sharp knife

Cut watermelon into 1 inch slices. Cut slices into triangles. Sit in the grass and eat until you're full up and your face and arms and legs are sticky, then go jump in the lake and swim awhile.

 Nuts and seeds, shelled or not, keep longer in the freezer.
They crack easier when frozen, too. And taste good on a hot day.
So do frozen grapes.

Family Reunion

· · · · · · · · · · · · · ·

Pink Dip

Pepperoni Pasta Salad

Frozen Fruit Dessert

Mounds Bars

Rhubarb Custard Cake

Made rhubarb custard cake on Saturday, and it was pretty good. We had just come off a merciless heat wave and I spent a good part of the afternoon doing some yard work I'd neglected in the 100-plus heat. Nothing challenging, and a lovely thing to pull weeds and move rocks around without feeling I'm going to pass out. And with the radio playing in the garage and a raspberry orange smoothie in a glass on the window ledge, I was feeling as if my back yard was Good Times Central. Bare feet and all.

It's not always that way. Now and then the kids remind me of a feeling I used to have pretty frequently but don't so much anymore. If it doesn't have a long German word for its name, it ought to: that feeling that everyone else in the world is having fun and you're not included. The kids never actually say it that way; no one ever really says, "The party is out there, and I'm not." But I think we all feel it. I know I've felt it, in the middle of the night, or doing laundry while managing three toddlers, while I'm bagging my groceries, while I'm sitting on the porch.

Maybe it's a way we feel sorry for ourselves when we're lonely, or doing something we'd rather not do. Or perhaps it's a story we tell ourselves to distract ourselves from responsibility for our own lives. I like to think that we're simply not paying attention. It's about perspective, and attitude, and most of us don't get a grip until we've had some experiences that make us appreciate things. Because, if you are like me, you've noticed that feeling shows up less and less as you grow older. More and more, I think to myself, "This is where the party is." It happens when I'm folding laundry, baking a pie, in church, or eating pancakes at the café with a friend who just returned from Vancouver, or strolling around a lake holding hands with Mr. Sundberg on an afternoon when the sun feels warm but not hot and there's a loon calling and I smell hot dogs and popcorn. I don't concern myself with the Big Party out there, because I've always been there. Just maybe on the fringe at a table with a candle near a window or out in the parking lot looking at the moon. Now I'm on the Planning Committee. I've a say about the menu, and the karaoke machine is in working order. Whether I sing or not is up to me, and I'm thinking I will. The "Day-O" song. Or maybe, "Somewhere Over the Rainbow." Who knows. Gonna be a party is what I do know, and I've got a lifetime invitation.

Pink Dip

8 oz cream cheese
1 T grated onion
1 tsp lemon juice
1 tsp Worcestershire sauce
A bit of ketchup to pinken it up a bit

Mix all ingredients together with a wooden spoon, and serve with your favorite plain potato chips.

Pepperoni Pasta Salad

1 large pkg seashell macaroni
1 can small black olives, drained
1 jar green olives, drained
1 pkg sliced pepperoni
1 small red onion, sliced and halved
8 oz (or so to taste) cubed mozzarella cheese
¼ cup oil
½ cup red wine vinegar
Oregano, basil, garlic, parsley, rosemary, salt, and pepper to taste
Fresh grated Parmesan cheese

Cook pasta; drain and cool. Combine all ingredients with pasta, except Parmesan cheese. Toss in oil and vinegar. Add herbs and salt and pepper to taste. Sprinkle Parmesan on top.

Frozen Fruit Dessert

1 cup sugar

2 cups water

2 (10 oz) packages frozen strawberries

1 (6 oz) can frozen orange juice concentrate

1 (6 oz) can frozen lemonade concentrate

1 small jar maraschino cherries and juice

1 small can crushed pineapple and juice

4 bananas, cut up

Cook 1 cup sugar and 2 cups water until sugar is dissolved. Add strawberries while water is hot. Add remaining ingredients, except bananas. Finally, add 4 cut up bananas. Stir gently. Freeze in a 9x13 pan. Cut into squares and serve in small bowls.

Mounds Bars

2 cups graham cracker crumbs

½ cup butter, melted

⅓ cup sugar

2 cups flaked coconut

1 can sweetened condensed milk

2 cups semi-sweet chocolate chips

1 T shortening

Mix first three ingredients in 9x13 pan. Bake 5 minutes at 300.

Combine coconut and sweetened condensed milk, and spread over cooled crumb crust. Bake 15 minutes at 325. Melt together chocolate chips and shortening, and pour and spread over cooled coconut layer. Refrigerate until chocolate is firm. Let sit on counter a short while before cutting.

Rhubarb Custard Cake

1 box yellow cake mix
4 cups diced rhubarb
1 cup sugar (I use ¾ cup)
1 pint whipping cream

Mix cake according to the directions on the box. Pour into a greased 9x13 pan. Cover the batter with the rhubarb. Sprinkle the sugar over. Pour the whipping cream over the top.

Bake 55 to 60 minutes at 350. Serve warm.

Dog Days Afternoon

Cool Cucumber Sandwiches

Barbecued Chicken Wraps

Spinach Salad with Bacon

Drumstick Dessert

Mrs. Sundberg's Good-and-Good-For-Ya
Chocolate Chip Cookies

Made cucumber sandwiches on Saturday, and they were pretty good. It's been a busy summer so far with the kids' activities and driving here and there and Mr. Sundberg's speaking engagements taking up a good deal of his time. He comes and goes and in between works on his chainsaw carvings and the stone wall he's building out back, and, once in a while, he takes a break and sits in a chair and lets out a big sigh and smiles. "How ya doin'?" he says, and drinks his iced tea, and I say, Fine, and you? And he nods and taps the table with his glass and smiles some more like his life is something else.

It's good to have things to do, and it's good to sit and do nothing sometimes, too. Though I have a hard time with that, as I always want to be doing something. Gives the hours meaning, you know, to fill them with something as opposed to nothing. Though nothing can be something if you're in need of fillin' up.

Like this weekend. I'm taking off for a retreat, a kind of women's thing where you gather at a farm in the middle of nowhere and sit in a circle and tell stories and write about your life and laugh and cry, and then you go off on your own and write some more and cry some more and fall asleep doing so, and when you wake up the sun is setting and you smell a campfire and hear voices and birds and think you might be in heaven but it's really as close as you're gonna get for a while. They might call it a "retreat" but I'm thinking my mother is right. It's recreation. Not water-skiing and rock climbing and boating and all that, but "re-creation" in its most literal sense. You go away awhile to re-create yourself and it's a thing worth its while. Some people carve bears out of wood. Others meditate nude in the center of a meadow. Me? I take a road trip, find some people to share stories with, and fall asleep writing. No socks to wash, no dishes, no children hollering, "He licked me!" Sounds like a good time to me. Sure does.

Cool Cucumber Sandwiches

8 oz cream cheese, softened
1 pkg dry ranch dressing mix
1-2 T milk
1 loaf white bread, crusts removed (or a baguette works, too)
1 cucumber, peeled if you wish, and sliced thin

Mix the cream cheese and ranch dressing mix, adding milk as needed to make it easy to spread.

Depending on how much time you want to spend on these, you can just spread slices of bread with cream cheese mixture, cut in quarters and top with cucumber slices. The kids like to cut circles out of the bread, then spread with cream cheese mixture and top with cucumbers. If I'm using a baguette, I just slice, spread, top.

For color, you can add a strip of red pepper or pimento, or a sprinkle of paprika.

Barbecued Chicken Wraps

1 lb boneless chicken breasts
1-2 T oil
Salt and pepper, to taste
1 (18 oz) bottle of your favorite barbecue sauce
6-8 flour tortillas or soft pitas
8 oz shredded cheddar cheese

Trim fat from chicken. Place in skillet with 1-2 T oil. Fry on both sides until there isn't much pink to be seen. While in skillet, cut breasts in half and shred with two forks. Continue to cook over medium heat until pink is gone. Season with salt and pepper. Pour one bottle of barbecue sauce over meat. Simmer 20 minutes. Scoop onto warm pita or tortilla. Sprinkle with desired amount of shredded cheese and roll up or fold. Wrap in foil if you're heading out for a picnic.

Use Ziploc bags when marinating meats and such. This way, you can massage the contents without opening the bag, and cleanup is quick.

Spinach Salad with Bacon

Dressing

½ cup packed brown sugar
½ cup salad oil
⅓ cup vinegar
⅓ cup ketchup
1 T Worcestershire

Salad

2 qt fresh spinach leaves, torn
1 (16 oz) can bean sprouts, drained, or 2 cups fresh sprouts
1 (8 oz) can water chestnuts, drained
4 hard-boiled eggs, peeled and sliced
6 slices of bacon, fried and crumbled
1 small onion, thinly sliced

Combine dressing ingredients in jar or plastic container with lid and shake well. Set aside.

Toss salad ingredients in a large bowl. Just before serving, pour dressing over salad and toss. Serves 8.

Drumstick Dessert

5 cups Cocoa Krispies cereal
¾ cup peanut butter
¾ cup light corn syrup
½ gallon of vanilla ice cream
1 cup crushed peanuts, more if desired
Chocolate syrup

Mix first three ingredients. Pat into lightly greased 9x13 pan. Spread ½ gallon of vanilla ice cream over mixture. Sprinkle with crushed dry roasted peanuts. Drizzle with chocolate syrup. Cover with foil and freeze.

Mrs. Sundberg's Good-and-Good-for-Ya Chocolate Chip Cookies

1 cup butter
1 cup white sugar
1 cup brown sugar
2 eggs
1 tsp vanilla
2 cups flour
2½ cups blended oatmeal (I use a blender to pulverize the oatmeal; adjust coarseness to your liking)

½ tsp baking powder
1 tsp baking soda
1 cup chocolate chips (2 cups if you're hardcore about chocolate)

Cream together butter and sugars; add eggs and vanilla and stir well. Add dry ingredients, and mix, and stir in chocolate chips.

Drop by the spoonful onto ungreased cookie sheet, and bake for 6-7 minutes at 375. Makes about 60 cookies.

Evening Fiesta Out on the Deck

· · · · · · · · · · · · · ·

Bean and Corn Salsa Dip

Taco Salad

Chicken Cornchiladas

Mrs. Sundberg's "Fried" Ice Cream

Made taco salad on Saturday, and it was pretty good. After a long week of school shopping and supply buying and loading up on after-school snacks and answering questions about school and what bus and how many more days . . . Saturday felt like Saturday. I spent a good part of the morning talking with people—on the phone with a salesperson, and with someone handing out tracts door to door. Some people you meet only once in your life and nothing wrong with kindness and a good ear.

Been a lot of high emotion these August days with the heat and all, and storm systems rolling in, and the rush to get it together before school begins. My comment Saturday afternoon at the grocery store got a laugh from the woman working at the deli: "Guess the Good Mood Club canceled their meeting today." Easy to forget that every person is a life, with a bazillion relatives who each have their own lives. And every life is full up with every facet of what it means to be a human being on Earth: issues financial, marital, parental, social, job-related, religious, political, global, personal. So much. On top of all of that, we have beds to make, clothes to coordinate, food to cook, pets to manage, and a real need for a hearty laugh now and then, and a deep conversation, and a good long hug.

Dropped the kids off at school this morning for orientation, and they didn't want to hug me. Too many other kids around, maybe, for the awkwardness of leaning over the seat or into the car. Which is OK. They hugged me last night, each of them, before bed. "A Real One," I said, and they each came through. I got three solid embraces, felt their hearts beating and the warmth of their skin, smelled their hair.

Easy to forget, in all the rush, in all of the pain and anxiety and tumult, in the quiet and the clamor of the doorbell and Aisle 4 and in the waiting room at the car repair shop how important it is to touch each other, to pause just for a moment and wrap our arms around a person we love and feel the beat of a heart other than our own. So here's my charge this time around: Hold someone close to you today, someone you love or could love, or someone who drives you up a wall but you're going to give it a whirl anyway. If nothing else, it's a shot of endorphins. Which we all need. And I find, often, when I need something, I give it. Just sayin'.

Bean and Corn Salsa Dip

1 can corn, drained
1 can black beans, rinsed and drained
1 jar of your favorite salsa (homemade is good)

Mix above three ingredients and chill. Serve with tortilla chips and sour cream. Great as an appetizer or a last-minute snack to bring along to a party. And kids love this one.

Taco Salad

1 lb hamburger, fried and drained and seasoned with taco seasoning
1 head lettuce, chopped
4 green onions
2 chopped tomatoes
1 can dark red kidney beans
8 oz grated cheddar
16 oz Kraft Creamy Italian Light dressing (or similar dressing)
12 oz bag Nacho Cheese Doritos

Layer in above order, except for Doritos. Refrigerate. Crush Doritos over.

Chicken Cornchiladas

1 pkg boneless chicken breasts (20 oz)
1 T oil
Salt and pepper
1 pkg taco seasoning
¾ cup of water
1 can whole kernel corn, drained
3 cups shredded cheddar cheese
1 (30 oz) can enchilada sauce
1 pkg large tortillas (10)

Trim fat from chicken, cut breasts into thirds and place into a large skillet with 1 T or so of oil and some salt and pepper. Fry on medium heat, both sides. As meat cooks, pull it into shreds with two large forks. When chicken is cooked through (even a bit golden brown is nice), add taco seasoning and ¾ cup or so of water. Stir. Add corn. Stir. Add 1 cup shredded cheese.

Mix and let simmer 10 minutes or so on low. Remove from burner. Pour enough enchilada sauce into a 9x13 pan to coat the bottom. Place 2-3 large spoonsful of chicken mixture into each tortilla shell. Roll and press into pan. Pour remainder of enchilada sauce over rolled tortillas, and sprinkle 2 cups shredded cheddar over. Bake at 350, uncovered, 30 minutes or to your liking. Let sit 5 minutes before serving. For variety, try adding a can of drained black beans to the filling along with the corn.

Mrs. Sundberg's "Fried" Ice Cream

Your favorite granola (with cinnamon works best) or Cinnamon Toast Crunch cereal, crushed, is even better, or one of a variety of similar cereals

Vanilla ice cream, frozen

Honey

Cool Whip

Break or crush granola/cereal so there are no large chunks. Place in medium-sized bowl. Quickly shape ice cream into balls about the size of tangerines or billiard balls, and press into granola, rotating and pressing until the ice cream is completely covered. Place two of the ice cream balls in a bowl, drizzle honey over, and top with whipped cream and a sprinkle of cinnamon.

Enjoy!

Index

About the Author

At age 9, in the back seat of her grandmother's car on the way to a funeral, Holly Harden began to write, and she's been writing ever since. She grew up in several small Wisconsin towns, and majored in English and education at St. Olaf College in Northfield, Minnesota. After teaching English and literature at the secondary level for nine years, she earned an MFA in writing from Hamline University. Her nonfiction work has appeared in publications such as *Utne* and *Fourth Genre*, and most recently in the essay collection, *upon arrival of illness: coming to terms with the dark companion*. She is the editor for Garrison Keillor's *Life Among the Lutherans*, and lives in Minnesota, where she writes for *A Prairie Home Companion*, teaches writing classes and helps her three children get where they're going.

Photo by Tom Roster